Scriptures in Dialogue

Scriptures in Dialogue

Christians and Muslims studying the Bible and the Qur'ān together

A record of the seminar 'Building Bridges'
held at Doha, Qatar, 7–9 April 2003

Edited by Michael Ipgrave

CHURCH HOUSE PUBLISHING

Church House Publishing
Church House,
Great Smith Street,
London SW1P 3NZ

ISBN 0 7151 4012 4
GS Misc 726

Published 2004 by Church House Publishing

Printed in England by The Cromwell Press, Trowbridge, Wiltshire

Contents

Participants in the Christian–Muslim seminar at Doha,
Qatar 7–9 April 2003   vii

Introducing the seminar   ix

     His Highness Sheikh Hamad bin Khalifa al-Thani
     The Amir of the State of Qatar   ix

     The Most Revd and Rt Hon. Dr Rowan Williams   xi
     The Archbishop of Canterbury

     Michael Ipgrave   xii

Chapter 1   Muslims and Christians reading scriptures:
            When, where, how, with whom?   1

Chapter 2   Listening to God, learning from scripture   25

     On the road to Emmaus   25
     Tom Wright

     Listening to God through the Qur'ān   36
     Vincent Cornell

     Scripture dialogue I: Signs of God   43
     Psalm 19; al-Rūm (30) 19-30

     Readings of the 'Reading'   50
     Tim Winter

Scripture dialogue II: Word of God   55
Āl 'Imrān (3) 1-7; John 1.1-18

Chapter 3   Legacies of the past, challenges of the present   63

Scripture dialogue III: Abraham, a righteous man   63
Romans 4; al-Baqara (2) 124-36

The ethics of gender discourse in Islam   72
Mona Siddiqui

A Circle perspective   80
Esther Mombo

Scripture dialogue IV: Righteous women   93
al-Aḥẓab (33) 28-36; Proverbs 31.10-31

Chapter 4   Scripture and the Other   102

Christian scripture and 'the Other'   102
Frances Young

Affirming the self through accepting the Other   111
Basit Koshul

Scripture dialogue V: Space for the Other?   119
Jonah 3 and 4; al-Baqara (2) 62, Āl 'Imrān (3) 113-15
John 14.1-14; Āl 'Imrān (3) 19-20, 85

Christian theology and other faiths   131
Rowan Williams

Chapter 5   Scriptures in dialogue   144
Notes   147

Participants

Professor Muhammad Abdel Haleem

King Fahd Professor of Islamic Studies, School of Oriental and African Studies, University of London

Dr Salwa el-Awa

Lecturer in Islamic Studies, Department of Theology, University of Birmingham

Sheikh Dr Zaki Badawi

Principal, The Muslim College, London

The Revd Canon Dr Kenneth Bailey

Canon Theologian of the Episcopal Diocese of Pittsburgh, Pennsylvania

Professor Vincent Cornell

Director, King Fahd Centre for Middle East and Islamic Studies, University of Arkansas

Professor Ellen Davis

Associate Professor of Bible and Practical Theology, Duke Divinity School, Durham, North Carolina

The Most Revd Michael Fitzgerald

President, Pontifical Council for Interreligious Dialogue, Vatican City

Professor David Ford

Regius Professor of Divinity, University of Cambridge

Dr Ida Glaser

Senior Teaching and Research Fellow, Edinburgh Centre for Muslim-Christian Studies

Dr Riffat Hassan

Professor of Humanities and Religious Studies, University of Louisville, Kentucky

The Revd Canon Dr Michael Ipgrave

Inter Faith Relations Adviser, Archbishops' Council of the Church of England

Dr Assaad Kattan

Institute of History, Archaeology and Near Eastern Studies, University of Balamand, Lebanon

Dr Basit Koshul
University of Virginia and Lecturer in Comparative Religion, Concordia College, Moorhead, Minnesota

Dr Jane Dammen McAuliffe
Dean of Georgetown College, Georgetown University, Washington DC

The Revd Dr Daniel Madigan SJ
Director, Institute for the Study of Religions and Cultures, Pontifical Gregorian University, Rome

Dr Maleiha Malik
Lecturer in Law, King's College, University of London

Professor Mustansir Mir
University Professor of Islamic Studies, Youngstown State University, Ohio

Dr Esther Mombo
Academic Dean, St Paul's United Theological College, Limuru, Kenya

The Rt Revd Dr Michael Nazir-Ali
Bishop of Rochester

Dr Mona Siddiqui
Head of Department of Theology and Religious Studies, University of Glasgow

Professor Muhammad Suheyl Umar
Director, Iqbal Academy, Lahore

Mr Timothy Winter
Lecturer in Islamic Studies, Faculty of Divinity, University of Cambridge

The Most Revd and Rt Hon. Dr Rowan Williams
Archbishop of Canterbury

The Rt Revd Dr Tom Wright
Bishop of Durham

Professor Frances Young
Edward Cadbury Professor of Theology, University of Birmingham

Introducing the seminar

From 7–9 April 2003, 25 Muslim and Christian scholars gathered in Doha, Qatar, for a seminar convened by the Archbishop of Canterbury and hosted by the Amir of the State of Qatar. Their purpose was to explore the contribution which a joint reading of their scriptures, the Qur'ān and the Bible, could make to Christian–Muslim dialogue. This volume is intended to provide a record of their discussions.

The seminar was the second in a series entitled 'Building Bridges'. The first had been held at Lambeth Palace, London in January 2002 – a record of which was published as *The Road Ahead: A Christian–Muslim Dialogue* (ed. Michael Ipgrave; London: Church House Publishing, 2002). Like that earlier event, the Doha seminar involved Muslim and Christian contributions on a basis of equality and mutuality. It broke new ground in carrying out most of its work in small group discussions which focused on the reading side-by-side of biblical and Qur'ān passages. In addition, the programme included public lectures on paired themes by Muslim and Christian speakers, as well as plenary discussions.

The introductory material presented in this chapter includes the remarks of the Amir of the State of Qatar and of the Archbishop of Canterbury at the opening of the seminar and a note explaining the structure and status of the following chapters.

The Amir of the State of Qatar, His Highness Sheikh Hamad bin Khalifa al-Thani

There is no doubt that the convening of this seminar takes place under extremely difficult circumstances – namely the war now going on in our region. We have done our best to avert this war, and to limit its complications as much as possible. This grievous situation adds deep dimensions and noble meanings to this seminar since it is a meeting for the sake of peace and reviving the sublime values and ideals of both Islam and Christianity, which religions together believe in the oneness of the Almighty God, and call for fraternity, equality, tolerance, moderation, the rejection of violence, respect for human rights, and the maintenance of man's dignity, life and property. These sublime principles have for centuries formed the original common denominators between the two religions and cultures.

Perhaps it is useful to recall that the Holy Qur'ān ordered us not to argue with Jews and Christians except in the best and most gracious ways, and to preach the right path with wisdom and good advice. Therefore, we beseech God to bestow success on your work so that dialogue between civilizations overcomes the challenges and obstacles. We are quite sure that your high status and enlightened thoughts will address in this seminar the obstructions that hinder the course of civilized cooperation between the followers of the two faiths.

Perhaps among the most evident obstructions are two major problems: first, the diversion of the course of the heavenly religions from the essence of their message and manipulation of their tenets to serve political purposes; and secondly, passing judgement on a whole nation because of the behaviour of a minority of extremists or ignorant people, and so distorting its civilization, threatening its interests and offending its established principles. In our view, these are the two original causes of the distorted and false stereotypes of Islam and Christianity, which we see here and there, as portrayed by the media and propagated by racist writers, and which only serve to widen the gap between the followers of the two religions, and make discord replace harmony and clash replace dialogue.

In face of the turbulent events of recent times, we should not forget to point out that our Arab region is honoured by God the Almighty with the revelation of the messages of Moses and Jesus Christ, peace be upon them, and the daybreak of the Muhammadan message. The Arab-Muslims, Jews and Christians have lived together in peace, security and fraternity of faith, striving to excel in beneficence and common good. But the land of prophets has for half a century been suffering, and continues to suffer, from the lack of security, peace and stability, as a result of persistence of the Arab–Israeli conflict without a just settlement due to the absence of international legality. We look for much from this seminar, hoping that its discussions and papers would go deep into the roots of those obstructions, and find the effective mechanism to activate dialogue.

I would like to take this opportunity to propose the formation of a permanent body for dialogue between Islam and Christianity, to be based in Qatar. We believe in the significance of such dialogue between civilizations and in the principles of affection, tolerance and consultation among societies and nations, and will be honoured to contribute to the efforts aimed at deepening understanding and promoting rapprochement and cooperation among Muslim and non-Muslim countries.

Peace, mercy, and the blessings of God.

The Archbishop of Canterbury, The Most Revd and Rt Hon. Dr Rowan Williams

My first duty, which I discharge with the most sincere pleasure, is to thank His Highness the Amir of Qatar for welcoming us to his country and doing so much to facilitate this meeting. From earlier days when my predecessor was welcomed here, His Highness has shown exemplary commitment to this dialogue and has pursued it with an energy and vision characteristic of all he has done as ruler of this small but rapidly evolving country. He has shown precisely the kind of enthusiasm for honest exchange and deepened understanding which meetings such as this are designed to assist, and we are all profoundly grateful. It is a kind of openness that is also making possible significant gestures towards the Christian community here, and for that too let me express my gratitude.

I have mentioned my predecessor, and I cannot let the opportunity go past of paying tribute to the courage and imagination with which he addressed these issues of mutual understanding across the frontiers of our communities of faith. I hope to continue such work, conscious all the time of doing no more than building on foundations which he laid through much labour, much thought and prayer, and much tireless fostering of relationships in many lands.

For many, a real dialogue about what we specifically believe and the thoughts we have about our faith ought to take second place to discussions concerning the practical tasks we can share, whatever our faith – and this is thought to be especially true at a time of tension. But this dialogue has been conceived rather differently. Christians are Christians and Muslims are Muslims because they care about truth, and because they believe that truth alone gives life. About the nature of that absolute and life-giving truth, Christians and Muslims are not fully in agreement. Yet they are able to find words in which to explain and explore that disagreement because they also share histories and practices that make parts of their systems of belief mutually recognizable – a story reaching back to God's creation of the world and God's call to Abraham; a practice of reading and absorbing scriptures and of shaping a life in response to the Word God speaks to creation.

We are here to discover more about how each community believes it must listen to God, conscious of how very differently we identify and speak of God's revelation. It is a significant meeting not primarily because it coincides with a time of such conflict and anxiety but because it highlights again a deeper and abiding need – a need which the run-up to this present conflict has made all the more urgent.

Listening to God and listening to one another as nations, cultures and faiths have not always had the priority they so desperately need. So this space for reflection is all the more important; it is both a symbol and an example of this kind of engagement.

In this dialogue, we are not seeking an empty formula of convergence or trying to deny our otherness; indeed, as we reflect on the holy texts we read, we shall be seeking to make better sense of how we relate to the other, the stranger with whom we can still speak in trust and love. As we do this – experience shows us – we learn more of the depths of what nourishes us in our own faith; and we hope to go from this dialogue better equipped to witness in a deeply troubled world, to witness to what faith and humble obedience to God and patient attention to each other might have to offer to struggling and suffering nations throughout the globe.

Michael Ipgrave

The Doha Christian–Muslim seminar was held from 7–9 April 2003. On the three working days of the programme, the following general themes were addressed in turn: 'Listening to God, learning from scripture'; 'Legacies of the past, challenges of the present'; and 'Scripture and the other'. Each day's programme included two public lectures, the texts of which are included in Chapters 2–4 of this book. These chapters also aim to provide some record of the major part of the seminar's work, which was carried out in four parallel small groups, each composed of Christian and Muslim scholars. These groups met on a total of six occasions for intensive reading of paired passages from the Qur'ān and the Bible. Participants were greatly assisted in this study process by notes on the scriptural passages prepared by Kenneth Bailey, Vincent Cornell, Ellen Davis, Salwa el-Awa, Muhammad Abdel Haleem, Esther Mombo and Tom Wright; many of these scholars' insights appear in the pages which follow.

It is of course not at all possible to convey here the detailed insight, the depth and breadth, or the variety and nuance of these text-based group discussions. In the five sections entitled 'scripture dialogues', I have tried to summarize and collate some of the key themes emerging from the groups; inevitably, however, this is a partial and personal record, and I take full editorial responsibility for any inadvertent omissions or distortions which may have occurred.

The first and last chapters of this book are based on material provided by participants before and after the seminar. Chapter 1 presents their richly varied responses to the question: 'When, where, how and with whom do I read scripture?' Chapter 5 seeks to identify some of the learning points from the seminar process as a whole; I have drawn particularly on material supplied by David Ford for this chapter.

I am very grateful to Jane McAuliffe, David Marshall and Ellen Davis for their detailed comments on draft manuscripts of this text, and to them and several others for help in correcting my often erratic Arabic transliterations; any remaining mistakes are entirely my fault. Biblical texts quoted in the scripture dialogues are from the New Revised Standard Version. The corresponding Qur'ānic passages are cited in an English translation provided by Muhammad Abdel Haleem which was used in the seminar groups. I am very grateful to him for permission to use these texts drawn from his forthcoming translation of the entire Qur'ān.

Chapter 1

Muslims and Christians reading scriptures: When, where, how, with whom?

A 'dialogue of scriptures' can only be generated through a dialogue of the readers of those scriptures. This in turn means that the possibility of scriptural dialogue between Christians and Muslims must be built on the prior reality of a dialogue of the scriptures with their respective communities – an engagement with the Bible on the part of Christians, and with the Qur'ān on the part of Muslims. This chapter brings together some personal reflections on these foundational dialogues through which God addresses believers of either faith through their scriptures. Twenty contributors (thirteen Christians, seven Muslims) supply their own answers to the question: 'When, where, how and with whom do I read scripture?' Their responses demonstrate the many levels at which this personal engagement take place, and underline the centrality of scripture for individuals and communities in both traditions.

Muhammad Abdel Haleem

My engagement with the Qur'ān goes back to my childhood when I had to learn it by heart to qualify for entry to al-Azhar's education in Arabic and Islamic Studies. For nine years in al-Azhar schools we had to take an oral examination at the end of each year to ensure that we still knew the Qur'ān by heart – and it was a matter of pass or fail in those days. The Qur'ān was central in our studies there; even grammar rules have to be given bases for their validity from the Qur'ān.

My father, God rest his soul, made me promise that I would read some Qur'ān every day, and I have kept to this. I read from beginning to end, now finishing it, on average, about once a month. This is an easy task: it is not really a long book and I know it by heart. I could read it to myself from memory on a bicycle in Cambridge and now, in London, I can do it on the underground. My promise, made in an Egyptian village many decades ago is now kept on the British transport system – in a global village! In my mind's eye I see words and verses in their specific positions on each page as I read it, and that is why I keep to the King

Fu'ad Egyptian edition of fifteen lines per page, from which I learned as a child. This exercise hopefully helps me to keep my brain and memory active, and gives me an opportunity to reflect on the words, if I am not reciting at fast-forward. When life becomes oppressive, I play tapes of good recitations, and intone the Qur'ān to myself, letting the words, style and music of the Arabic text lift my mood.

I teach different aspects of the Qur'ān to my students at SOAS, I write on it, I give talks on it, and I edit an academic journal about it. I quote the Qur'ān when I give expert evidence on some aspects of Islamic law in courts – lucrative, and it seems to impress British judges! Like other practising Muslims everywhere I recite some Qur'ān in the five daily prayers, mainly with the family, who keep asking me questions about it, and Muslims who know my specialization do the same.

Over the last few years I have been working on producing a new translation of the Qur'ān into English – now completed, thank God! During this exercise I was regularly reminded of the good advice of Professor Anne Lambton, my outstanding Head of Department many years ago, who counselled teachers on supervising research students and said once: 'We should get students to translate some passages, which they consult in Arabic, Persian, etc., for only then would they come to realize how much they knew of it and how much they did not really know.' The process of translation has certainly enhanced my understanding of the Qur'ān and made me more open to people of other religions. I think that perhaps a seminar should be arranged to examine how translations and interpretations can help or hinder inter faith dialogue.

Reflecting on these questions has made me wake up and become even more aware of the centrality of the Qur'ān in my life – a joyful and awesome responsibility.

Kenneth Bailey

I grew up in Egypt with a British mother (Church of England) and an American father (Presbyterian). Scripture was read aloud every evening by my father as part of family prayers throughout my early years.

Three of my six years of postgraduate study focused on the New Testament, with special emphasis on the parables of Jesus. Two years of full-time Arabic study in Cairo made it possible for me to begin a life-long investigation of the 120-year-old tradition of translations of the New Testament into Arabic from Greek, Coptic and Syriac. I taught New Testament for forty years in the Middle East (in Arabic and in English) and now for seven years have continued writing and lecturing in the same field in North America, Europe, the Middle East and Asia. Opportunities to lecture are extended to me from Anglicans, Presbyterians, Roman Catholics and Lutherans. The seminars I lead are largely continuing education events for priests.

My ongoing research and writing continues to focus on an attempt to better understand the person and sayings of Jesus in the light of the culture of the Middle East. The great Arab interpreters of the Gospels, such as Musa bar Kefah (ninth century, Iraq), Hibitallah Ibn al-'Assāl (thirteenth century, Egypt) and 'Abdallah Ibn al-Tayyib (eleventh century, Iraq) are among the primary sources for this quest, along with the early Syriac and Arabic translations of the first twelve hundred years of Christian history.

This quest is not merely an academic exercise. I pray five times each day. The evening prayers include readings from the Christian scriptures. Hardly a day passes without my reading up to ten chapters from the Bible. Only ill health keeps me from community prayers on Sunday. Throughout my life the Christian scriptures have been at the heart of who I am, what I seek to do and what I strive to become.

Ellen Davis

Since I am an Old Testament scholar employed as a teacher, my most self-conscious and time-consuming practice of reading scripture is done in the context of class-work, and secondarily in the writing that comes out of my teaching. My current job title designates my area of specialization as 'Bible and Practical Theology'; it is an accurate indicator of the kind of interest with which I read scripture. Specifically, I am concerned with three closely-related things:

1. theological exegesis;

2. the history of interpretation of the Bible among both Jews and Christians;

3. present possibilities for more profound and probing use of the Bible in the Church.

The relationship among these three lines of investigation is reflected in my current research projects, which focus on use of the Old Testament in preaching and also in formulating a Christian understanding of and response to the ecological crisis.

The other primary context in which I read and hear scripture is liturgical, in Sunday services (and other occasional services) at my parish church and in daily chapel services at Duke Divinity School. The readings for these services follow set lectionaries, which means they represent a selective reading of biblical books rather than a sequential one. While each lectionary may have a limited sequentiality, the fact that different services follow different lectionaries means that the total effect is quite patchy. Nonetheless, I often find that in the course of a day, a passage or even a phrase I heard or read in the liturgy becomes recontextualized in relation to questions I am considering and also to other texts that I may be studying (for teaching or writing) in more ordered fashion. Of course, the history of biblical interpretation witnesses to countless examples of just this kind of recontextualizing and (to use an old term for the phenomenon) 'collating' of texts. The liturgy is itself to a great extent a collation of biblical passages and phrases, and I am often aware that regular participation in the daily offices and the eucharistic liturgy creates a certain filter or lens through which I hear or view scripture altogether.

Finally, there are a couple of miscellaneous things I would like to note with respect to my reading of scripture. First, Hebrew is to my ears a language that is not only peculiarly expressive but also deeply engaging, and I find myself restive when I read or hear the text exclusively in English – so, for instance, I normally bring a Hebrew Bible to worship. Secondly, for my own private reading of scripture, for devotion or in times of difficulty, the Psalter is almost invariably the place to which I turn.

Salwa el-Awa

My relationship with the scripture, as captured in the four parts of the question 'where, when, how and with whom?', is one that is deeply rooted in many aspects of my relationship with my career, my family and myself.

My personal and individual relation with the Qur'ān has typical and individual aspects. I share the typical aspects with several million believers around the world; the particular aspects are those by which I believe I was advantaged, which were the fruits of the care of my father, my teachers and the outcome of my research.

The typical aspect is that of having the Qur'ān as a companion throughout the day and night: from the dawn, when I read it in my first daily prayer; in the morning, when I do my morning home work, having the Qur'ān played in the background, continuously reflecting on what it tells me about the world and about myself; through the day, with every subsequent prayer; through my work time, when I resort to it in my coffee breaks, following the most stressful moments of my working day, or when I move my eyes around the walls of my office or living room to read over and again the decorated Qur'ānic phrases hung on my walls, reflecting over and again on what insights they can add to my thinking about the day.

At evening times, parts of which I spend with my husband and our one-year-old son, reading the Qur'ān to him and to each other, reliving my father's tradition, making my son listen to the sound that we admire most and that touches me most, while in my thoughts and hopes I fantasize about how and when I will start teaching it to him as he grows up, and that is when I will do exactly what my father did for his children: help them devote a time for reciting the Qur'ān in their every day, ensure that they pronounce every letter and every word with just the right tone, stress and intonation, and draw their attention to the meanings of the Qur'ān, the stories, the personal prayers, the differences between the characters, the behaviour of different people, the leaders and the nations, the praise and glory of God, and the rhetoric and the amazing simplicity of the grammar which produces intriguingly complex meanings.

At an intellectual level, my experience with the scripture becomes more peculiar and individual. I am not exaggerating when I say that I almost never stop thinking about the Qur'ān. Everything that happens recalls a Qur'ānic verse to my mind, and I do just as I saw my teachers, Bint al-Shati', Lutfy fi Abdul-Badifi and Muhammad Abdel Haleem, do: I murmur verses in response to events or scenes that capture my mind, or recite them to whoever is present. Every verse I think of has a linguistic aspect that I make some initial thoughts about; sometimes these thoughts are developed in conversations with my father, my teachers or my students; sometimes they are developed into pieces of research, which I write and, sometimes, publish.

Such exercises have marked my teenage years, right through to the present day, often, especially during the early years, in pursuit of the question 'Why has the Qur'ān been considered inimitable?' It did not suffice that the ancestors have believed and said so, and it did not feel right that such a judgement should only be derived from belief: a method and a theory should be discovered or otherwise developed to enable the researcher or interpreter to investigate this statement in the language of this text.

A crucial point in my career was when I chose the topic of my MA thesis (which was a 100,000-word-long thesis in accordance with the Egyptian higher education system). It was meant to be an experiment based on the hypothesis that a correct understanding of the meaning would be incomplete without consideration of its context. I chose the multiple meaning words in the Qur'ān as an example of how context changes what we understand from the text. Then, I was most concerned with the immediate context. I enjoyed this work to such an extent that, as I was writing up the final chapter, I found myself praying to God never to deprive me of the joy of studying and explaining to others how The Book ought to be understood – a prayer which has been heard.

Shortly afterwards, my career was established as a teacher and researcher who endeavours to increase awareness of the role of the linguistic tool in understanding the Qur'ān, both as a whole and in parts, as a text, on the basis of modern linguistic theories.

In recent years, and especially after completion of my PhD thesis on textual relations within the Qur'ānic *sūra*, the hypothesis matured and turned into a profound intellectual conviction, that the intended meaning cannot possibly be recovered without reference to contextual information.

This continues to be the dominant theme of my teaching, reading and writing. However, my most recent experience of the Qur'ān, as a believer, is of uttering Qur'ānic verses in deep pain at the sight of the shocking pictures of victims of the war which keep coming through my mail. These verses feel as if they provide me with the only thing I can do to ease the pain, that is, to talk to God through his words: as if the Scripture is the magic spell that will restore peace in the world. If it does not, it does restore it in my heart, for a little while, at least.

Michael Fitzgerald

There are three ways in which the Scriptures come into my life: in liturgical prayer, in private prayer and in community prayer that is not liturgical.

In the Catholic liturgical prayer the Scriptures play a prominent role. In every Eucharist at least two passages are read out, and on Sundays and important feast days there are three readings. The final reading is always from one of the four Gospels. The other readings may be from the First Testament or from other books of the New Testament. The first reading is always followed by a passage from a psalm. The readings vary according to the liturgical season – Advent, Christmas, Lent, Easter, Pentecost, and what is called Ordinary Time. A good amount of the Bible is proclaimed in this way. As I am often the chief celebrant at the Eucharist, I am expected to comment on these readings. In order to do this, I have to read them over beforehand, reflect on them, sometimes look at commentaries on the passages for the day, pray about the texts, and then convey a message. I will do this almost always when celebrating with a community, even if the words said are very brief. I find that this stimulates my own prayer life.

In private prayer I sometimes, but not always, take a passage from the scriptures as a starting point. At times some word may strike me in a particular way and I find it is good to dwell on it. At other times, when the scripture passage is describing a scene, I may imagine myself taking part in the action. The scripture then shows me how I should be behaving. The scripture judges as well as comforts. My conviction is that the scripture has been inspired by the Holy Spirit, so that if I am in tune with the Spirit then the scriptures will speak to me.

Scripture is also used in non-liturgical community prayer, especially what is known in Christian circles as charismatic prayer. A passage from the Bible may be chosen at random, and yet still it will be found to have a message for this community or for some member(s) of the community. A passage may be chosen because it is in harmony with what has developed within the prayer meeting. Here again there is the conviction that the Holy Spirit is leading the prayer but making use of human cooperation to do so.

One further use of scripture is in the motto that I chose when ordained as a bishop. I selected two words from Psalm 1: *fructum dabit* – that is, 'It will give fruit.' The passage in full is: 'The just man is like a tree planted by running water; it will give fruit in due time.' This for me sums up the idea of dialogue, which will may produce fruit, though only if the conditions are right, and not without the exercise of some patience.

David Ford

It surprises me how various are the ways I engage with scripture: every Sunday worshipping with my family in St Benet's, Cambridge, where the Eucharist (whose whole liturgy is pervaded with scripture) always has an Old Testament and two New Testament readings, and a psalm, and the sermon usually tries to refer to all the readings; every day praying one daily office, using the Common Lectionary, sometimes with time for meditation; reading, writing and teaching Christian theology; occasional preaching, lecturing, and leading conferences or Bible studies; participating for the past seven years in the Society for Scriptural Reasoning, a group of Jews, Christians and Muslims who study our scriptures in dialogue with each other and have met annually at the American Academy of Religion, but also now increasingly elsewhere in between those meetings (a small Scriptural Reasoning group also meets every few weeks in Cambridge); a group of Christian graduate students and academics in the Cambridge Faculty of Divinity meeting regularly for 'Biblical Reasoning', inspired by Scriptural Reasoning and feeding into it; and various more occasional gatherings for study or meditation. My most sustained engagement with one text was five years of work on a book on meaning and truth in 2 Corinthians in intensive discussion with Frances Young as co-author, all sparked off by a remark that my favourite text was 2 Corinthians 4.6.

I find myself becoming more convinced and more passionate about the centrality of scripture both for Christian faith and practice and for inter faith engagements. A key idea at present is 'the wisdom interpretation of scripture', meaning interpretation that tries, alone or in a group setting, to take account of various methods, levels of meaning, and traditions of interpretation, while responding to current questions, situations and events, and living before God as the embracing context. Two especially fruitful times for me are when one-to-one or group discussions go well, and when there is time alone to ruminate open-endedly over a text, with the possibility of moving into and out of study, prayer, meditation, writing down thoughts, and using commentaries. An illuminating recent discovery has been of the value of studying the Old Testament by reading the Septuagint (the Greek translation of Hebrew scriptures made by Hellenistic Jews and used by the early Christians). I am increasingly fascinated by the 'conversations of scripture with scripture' – those many resonances between different parts of scripture, above all between Old and New Testaments, but also within each testament.

One of the richest and most surprising experiences with scripture in recent years has been through the Scriptural Reasoning network mentioned above. It makes deep sense for the primary common practice between Jews, Christians and Muslims to be study of our scriptures together, but it is also an enormous challenge. My basic thought about taking it further is that, while each of our traditions has well-developed forms of collegiality focused on studying our own scriptures, between our traditions there is almost no collegiality in the study of our scriptures together. What might be the appropriate forms of collegiality?

Ida Glaser

As a young child, I heard the Bible stories at school, and was given a book of New Testament stories by a committed Christian friend of my parents. So, when I was six years old and my Jewish father was baptized, I wanted to be baptized with him. I then went to Sunday school and continued to hear the stories. When, in my early teens, I rethought my belief in God, the recognition that I remembered the Bible stories much more clearly than the many 'myths and legends' that I had read was an important influence. I then started to read the Bible seriously, for up to an hour before school every day. At first, I criticized it. Then, little by little, I found that it was criticizing me, and this led to the full commitment to Christ and, eventually, the acceptance of the Bible as the written authority on which the rest of my life has been founded.

It was during my student days that I first heard systematic Bible teaching, with the exhortation so to study and live it that I would have 'bibline blood'. I disciplined myself to read the whole Bible by not allowing myself to eat until I had done my reading each day. Since then, scarcely a day has passed which has not begun with the Bible. This personal reading has sometimes followed a devotional commentary or 'Bible reading notes', sometimes gone through a book at a time, sometimes been a few sentences in Hebrew or Greek (I have never become proficient in either!), and sometimes followed a 'read the Bible in one year' plan. Sometimes it focuses on a passage on which I plan to preach, or on a book or topic which I am studying for academic purposes, so that I can pray these things into my personal life before I teach them to others. Sometimes, I feel that God is clearly speaking to me through his word, but sometimes I am so tired that I can hardly concentrate.

I also hear the Bible through preaching, and through a variety of groups which read together. I have read and heard with others in many different contexts – with Christians of different cultures, and with people of different faiths and none. At present, we are reading Luke's Gospel during our daily prayers at the Edinburgh Centre for Muslim–Christian studies – simply reading a passage, offering a few reflections, and then using it as a basis for our prayers. I am leading a small group at church, helping them to study Matthew's Gospel in the light of its historical context and literary structure. I am also working on a book that seeks to reread the whole Bible in the context of its interactions with the religions surrounding Israel, and therefore to discern more clearly how it leads Christians to understand and interact with people of other faiths today. I would like next to write a commentary on Genesis building on my doctoral studies, which read Genesis 1 – 11 in the context of parallel Qur'ānic stories.

I suppose that the greatest shift in my thinking over the years has been from a focus on doctrine and immediate personal guidance, in my teens and twenties, to an appreciation of the whole shape and story of the Bible, in recent years. I have increasingly reclaimed my Jewish heritage, and seen myself – and the rest of the world – as part of this great story of God's mission to his world through the Jewish people and ultimately through Christ. This is partly the result of reading the Bible alongside the Qur'ān, which has highlighted for me the difference in the way that the two books view history. While not having decreased my view of the authority of the Bible or my dependency on it for my personal relationship with God, I want to read it for what it is.

Michael Ipgrave

The first place each week where I read scripture – and where scripture is read to me – is as part of a congregation gathered for worship. On most Sundays, this is for me a group of about eighty people in an inner-city church in Leicester. The majority of them are people originally from the Caribbean islands of Barbados and Montserrat, who have found in this parish a spiritual home where they and their families can practise the dignified, liturgical Anglican Christianity they knew in the West Indies.

The scriptures in this church have an important place as a basis for teaching, for marking the key events in the cycle of the Christian year, and for consoling people who have known mostly hard lives with many experiences of poverty, isolation and discrimination. Particularly when I read passages in the Gospels which speak of God's promises to those who are burdened, I am very conscious of the way in which my understanding of these words is enriched by the lives of my fellow worshippers.

Because of the nature and location of my present employment, I commute some distance on most days of the week, taking an early train for a journey of an hour or so to London. This period of time provides the second regular time when I read scripture – I use the outward and return journeys to pray by myself the morning and evening prayers of the daily office (and also to read a daily newspaper). The structure of these offices gives me a regular diet from the book of Psalms, together with passages from both Testaments of the Bible. I find that the Psalms in particular, in their varied emotional moods, can help me to acknowledge and express the different, and often conflicting, dimensions of my self in the presence of God. At times, the reading of scripture according to a systematic daily plan can become a routine task, but then unexpectedly a particular phrase or image will seem to stand out from the page and remain with me for the rest of the day.

Although the daily office is an act of prayer shared across the Christian community, physically it can feel very much as if I am reading scripture entirely on my own as I sit in my railway carriage. Interestingly, however, I have noticed that many other people on the train from Leicester to London, and still more in the London underground, are reading to themselves religious books of various kinds – Christians reading Bibles or prayer books, but also Muslims, Hindus, Sikhs and others all using these moments of travel, away from other commitments, to read silently to themselves from religious texts. Sometimes, my eyes have looked up from my scriptures to catch the eyes of a fellow passenger looking up from his or her scripture of a different faith. Because we are in England and it is early in the morning, we would not presume to exchange words, but there is still perhaps a silent recognition that we are reading scriptures together in the same place; meanwhile, around us, other commuters tap away at spreadsheets and computer games on their laptops . . .

Assaad Kattan

My theological commitment took its 'mature' shape within the Orthodox Youth Movement, a prophetic Church organism/organ that has conduced in recent decades to a considerable theological and spiritual renewal of the Orthodox Church in Syria and Lebanon. Within the framework of this movement, it was self-evident to read the Bible and to comment on it in study groups thanks to an approach combining scientific exegesis, ethical questioning and spiritual insights.

In a further step, my theological studies enabled me to deepen this biblical 'interest' and to articulate questions pertaining to it more clearly. Furthermore, they offered me the opportunity to make the acquaintance of modern Western exegesis, especially the so-called 'historical-critical' method, and to reflect on its relevance for Orthodox theology, usually said to be conservative and little interested in modern theological issues.

Enriching in many respects as it was, however, the theological curriculum hardly provided a systematic and well-structured introduction to modern hermeneutical thought and a critical assessment of challenges raised by it. Students eager to widen their hermeneutical horizons with respect to the Christian scriptures were mostly dependent on personal efforts. In my case, ecumenical experiences and discussions helped me sharpen my hermeneutical sense.

In this respect, the encounter with Islam was of paramount importance due to the huge impact differences of interpretative premises and practices still exert even on daily life in the Near East, so shaping the way Christians and Muslims deal with each other. This urged me to dedicate more time in order to adequately grasp in their historical, cultural and hermeneutical logic those methods used by the Muslims to better understand their scriptures and to compare them with Christian interpretative ways.

Basit Koshul

The response to the questions 'when, where, how and with whom do I read scripture?' depends on the perspective from which the questions are being answered. The 'I' that engages scripture is not a static, abstract, conceptual being but rather a dynamic, concrete, sensuous becoming that is affected by, and is constantly called upon to respond to, an ever-changing, dynamic, concrete, sensuous environment. Consequently, the manner in which the 'I' engages scripture varies with the particular environment that the 'I' finds itself in at a particular time. I will discuss my engagement with scripture from three different perspectives: (a) the 'I' as individual believer; (b) the 'I' as a believer who is part of a community of believers; (c) the 'I' as an academician engaged in scholarly pursuits in the modern, secular academy. The fact that there appear to be multiple 'I's should not be taken to mean that they are seen as being mutually exclusive, but taken to understand that there is a reflexive relationship between the context in which scripture is being engaged and the text of scripture. In other words the 'how and with whom do I read scripture?' changes with the 'when and where' of the reading of scripture.

As an individual believer, scripture is at the centre of my liturgical life. It is not possible to complete the obligation of the five daily prayers without including scriptural passages from the Qur'ān in the prayer. Whereas one *sūra* from the Qur'ān must be a part of every prayer (i.e. *sūra al-Fātiḥa*, the very first *sūra*), the individual believer is given the option to include as much (or as little) of the Qur'ān in the daily prayers as he or she wishes. One is encouraged to include a substantial amount of scripture in the daily prayers beyond the mandatory passages because the recitation of scripture during the course of the daily prayer displays, affirms and renews the individual's relationship with God. At this level my engagement with scripture is very, very personal – expressing, and hopefully strengthening, my relationship with God.

As a believer who is part of a community of believers, I engage with scripture slightly differently. As a member of this community it is a part of my responsibility to ensure that scripture remains a living and vibrant entity in the community. In order to fulfil this responsibility, I make sure that my children learn how to read the Qur'ān in Arabic and also commit a portion of the Qur'ān to memory – continuing the tradition that began with Gabriel bringing the Qur'ān to Muhammad and having him commit it to memory. Outside the family, scripture is engaged with at the communal level when it comes to forming and shaping decisions regarding issues of communal concern. By turning to scripture for this particular purpose, the community does, or should, look at the manner in which earlier members of the community addressed similar issues of concern. At this level, scripture serves to bind the members of the faith community to each other, thereby bringing a community of believers into being. Practically speaking this happens in weekly 'Qur'ān study' sessions that are organized by members of the Muslim community of which I am a part. In this capacity, scripture not only binds those members who are present at a particular time and a particular place to each other; it also binds them to all those in all other times and places who have approached the Qur'ān with the same attitude and reverence.

As an academician working in the secular academy, I engage with scripture slightly differently than I do when inside the faith tradition. The basic reason for this different engagement is that I have become aware of certain questions and perspectives as a result of my training in the secular academy – questions and perspectives of which I never would have become aware if I had remained strictly within my religious tradition (or any religious tradition for that matter). My academic interests are focused on interrelating the social science of Max Weber with the theocentric semiotics of Charles Sanders Peirce and then relating this synthesis to the philosophy of religion articulated by Muhammad Iqbal. In the attempt to establish this interrelation, the Qur'ān is the alpha and the omega – the attempt has been inspired by the Qur'ānic narrative and it takes the narrative itself as the model of integration par excellence. In having undertaken this project I have had to open myself up to the interpretation of the Qur'ān being offered by people of other faith traditions (or even of no faith tradition) by virtue of the fact that I have offered the reading of the Qur'ān in this setting. At the same time I have had to open myself up to the study of the scriptures of other faith traditions, because I have realized that people from other faith traditions have attempted to use their own scriptures in similar ways. Even though it may not be readily apparent, I see this last context of reading scripture to be naturally related to the previous two contexts.

Jane Dammen McAuliffe

Although as a scholar of the Qur'ān I have published extensively on the Muslim scripture, I cannot claim a similar level of expertise in my own scripture, the Bible. While I have certainly paid some attention to biblical scholarship, particularly as it relates to or can provide an analogue to Qur'ānic studies, this attention has been focused more on matters of historiography and exegetical methodology than on textual content itself.

Last year I published a book with Oxford University Press that draws upon these comparative interests; I mention it primarily because of its title – *With Reverence for the Word: Medieval Scriptural Exegesis in Judaism, Christianity and Islam*. I chose the title because it so aptly captures the attitude which medieval scripture scholars in these three traditions brought to their study and textual treatment. It was a prayerful attitude, one that took the scripture in hand with a desire for both intellectual and spiritual nourishment. 'With reverence for the word' – that is the phrase that I hope characterizes my own approach, as a Christian, to the Bible. I rarely 'read' the Bible but I frequently 'pray' the Bible. For me, praying the Bible blends two spiritual disciplines, one long identified with the Benedictines, the other with the Jesuits.

The practice of *lectio divina* has deep roots in the Western monastic tradition. It is ordinarily understood to be the slow, reflective absorption of a small portion of the scriptural text. It is not reading for content so much as it is reading for resonance. Approaching the text with a prayerful attitude, one allows the words to sink in, to speak to the deepest layers of one's being, to become a living voice of the divine. *Lectio divina* runs counter to most other thrusts of my life; it pulls me to a profound quiet and renders superfluous any judgement of success or failure, of achievement or ineffectuality.

The reciprocal Jesuit discipline involves using the imagination to enter a biblical scene or narrative. Sometimes one adopts the role of interested bystander, while at other times one attempts to enter the mind and heart of a biblical character – Mary during the annunciation, Zacchaeus perched in a tree, Peter as he hears the cock crow. Imaginative entry into the story can bring one into the presence of the living Lord, collapsing that sense of remoteness that keeps Jesus from becoming a reality in one's hopes, fears and deepest desires.

I find that these two ways of praying the Bible are distinct but complementary. Some passages and some prayer periods seem more suited to one than the other. Usually I am drawn to the mode of *lectio divina* – probably because I cannot credit myself with a very good imagination – but this is not always so. Certain biblical scenes pull me in and an imaginative participation seems almost effortless.

And technology helps. A few years ago I bought a Palm Pilot to assist in the never-ending task of self-organization. Since this device doubles as an ebook reader it occurred to me to look for a Bible in electronic format. Eventually I located a King James version of the New Testament and then a Revised Standard Version of both testaments. Suddenly I found myself with a portable prayer room. The bright little screen focuses my attention at home or office and in planes, trains and taxis, blocking out surrounding distractions and opening a place of quiet presence. Because the screen displays only a few verses at a time, the temptation to speed ahead in the text is eliminated. The eyes rest on a small portion and the mind and heart either engage imaginatively with the scene presented or certain words and phrases begin to find an interior echo and the blessed conversation begins.

Daniel Madigan

Reflecting on the way in which I actually engage with scripture, I realize two important points: first, that I have quite different approaches to different parts of the text; and secondly, that much depends on which of my various roles is uppermost as I approach the text – theologian, preacher or individual believer coming to pray.

Like most people I would say that I work with a kind of 'canon within the canon'. Those parts of the Old Testament that I draw on most are the books of Genesis and Exodus, the prophets (especially Isaiah) and the Psalms. There are other parts, of course, but these books play the most important role. The first two books of the Pentateuch express in dramatic form the fundamental truths about God and humanity. Interestingly, perhaps even strangely for a Christian, the part of the

Bible which I sense most as the words of God directed to me are not from the New Testament but from the book of Isaiah the prophet – words of forgiveness, comfort, challenge and mission.

For me the Gospels function as a means, an entry point to a more imaginative and personal engagement with the figure of Jesus. I do not read them as simply the Word of God, but rather as words I know to have been handed down by the community of believers, written down and edited, put together in order to put me in contact with the Word that is Jesus. I know that of the many words written and spoken about Jesus, only these were eventually judged by the community to which I belong as reliable ways into contact with him. So my engagement with the Gospels is an attempt to place myself in the scene with him and explore it – listening, watching, sensing, responding. I recognize this is not the only way of approaching the text; I owe it principally to the tradition of Ignatius of Loyola in which I have grown up.

In preaching I am drawn beyond my personal choice of scripture passages and Gospel scenes. The texts are given to me and my task is to listen for the Word in them. My presumption is that the Word of God lies not so much in the words themselves as behind them. The words point us to the Word; but sometimes they can also obscure it. As a preacher my role is to hear the Word and make it resound, echoing in the hearts of those to whom I speak.

Esther Mombo

I was born and brought up as a programmed Quaker (not a silent congregation but one that has services which include singing, reading and preaching from the scriptures). The scriptures were very central in my life. My grandmother, who was among the first girls to become a Christian in her village, knew most of the Bible by heart. She told her grandchildren the biblical stories plus stories from her traditions. Each of the stories had a moral teaching behind it, whether it was an African story or a Bible story.

I heard stories about the Israelites: stories about baby Moses and how he was rescued and brought up; the Exodus story and all the miracles performed by Moses to convince the Pharaoh to allow them to leave Egypt; stories of the judges like Deborah, Samson and Delilah; the stories of young Samuel and his calling; the story of young David and how he became king. Being a widow, my grandmother loved the story of Ruth. From the New Testament she narrated the stories of the birth and life of Jesus, his arrest and crucifixion and resurrection. The stories of Paul's missionary journeys and how the churches were founded were very interesting. My grandmother told us, her grandchildren, these stories not for passing time but to help us come to know and have a faith in Jesus Christ so that we could join the church.

The stories, which my grandmother told me, were reinforced by Christian Religious Education classes at primary and secondary schools. In high school, I read the scriptures both as a subject in class and in the Christian union. This is when I made my commitment to become a Christian. This meant reading the scriptures for spiritual and moral guidance, following what was taught to me by my spiritual mentors.

When I began to study theology, I was introduced to methods of reading and interpreting scriptures and these began influencing me as I prepared to serve in the church. These methods included historical critical methods of exegesis, where the original meaning of the text was very important. However, other methods – such as women's readings of the Bible in different contexts – have had more impact on the way I read the Bible today. This way of reading the Bible takes note of the social context of the reader over and above the original context of the author.

I read the Bible for personal devotions, and with others in groups. I do not read the Bible as an answer book to every question that I have, but as a book which offers guidance in accordance with what God has spoken, especially through Jesus Christ. I read the Bible in community both in groups of intellectuals and with those who would not consider themselves intellectuals.

Mustansir Mir

I cannot claim to follow a systematic method of scriptural study. I do frequently read the Qur'ān – usually to study, with the help of exegetical literature, chapters and passages of the Qur'ān, often to look for answers to various types of questions that arise in the normal course of studying Islam or other religions, and sometimes to collect material for a talk on a Qur'ānic topic. As a rule, when I read the Qur'ān, I try to understand the meaning of the text in question, exploring the text's relationship with the preceding and following texts. In taking this approach, I have been influenced by the contemporary Qur'ānic exegete Amin Ahsan Islahi (d. 1997), whose Qur'ānic commentary, *Tadabbur-i Qur'ān* ('Reflection on the Qur'ān') I find to be invaluable. I hope some day to be able to produce, in English, a one- or two-volume abridgement of this multi-volume Urdu commentary. I like to note conceptual correspondences and verbal similarities in the

Qur'anic text, and I have tried to extend this interest of mine by reading classical – mostly pre-Islamic – Arabic poetry with the specific aim of determining the extent to which the language of the Qur'ān is similar to or different from the language of that poetry.

For the past few years, I have been holding weekly study sessions on the Qur'ān at one of the mosques in Youngstown, Ohio. I have noted that lecturing on the Qur'ān to a group of interested people comes to have a dynamic of its own. Such lecture or study sessions are often enriched by the unexpected introduction of new angles of looking at the Qur'ānic text. But this must be true of other scriptures as well.

Michael Nazir-Ali

I believe, along with many Christians, that the words and the form of the Bible are human but that the sense is of God. I try to read the Bible with both of these dimensions in mind. It is important, therefore, to give some time to reading the scriptures in the light of their historical, cultural and linguistic background. I do this as a matter of course in my preparation for preaching and other speaking engagements.

Scripture is also, of course, the Word of God, and we should not lose sight of this in any preparation we undertake. When we speak of the Bible as inspired we mean that it gives us information, which is reliable, about God's purposes for us and for the world. But we also mean that it has the capacity to inspire us personally and as communities in our daily living. From time to time, I read the Bible and hear it read in an atmosphere of meditation and reflection. This can sometimes be in the context of formal worship but it need not be that. Even contexts of worship can vary from a few people in chapel on a weekday morning to huge services with hundreds present. Each has its own value in terms of hearing God speak. Whenever God speaks, we cannot fail to be moved.

Sometimes, I read scripture with those who want to know more about it. Again, some want to know more about its historical and cultural background, while others are concerned particularly with the ways in which it addresses them as divine demand, love and acceptance. Such occasions for teaching are also, of course, opportunities for learning.

I read the Bible then in many different settings, always learning more about it and always learning from it.

Mona Siddiqui

As a Muslim, as an academic and as one interested in the study of religion, the reading of scripture has several layers of importance for me.

It has a personal dimension in which the reading of the Qur'ān carries a purely devotional significance; it also has an academic dimension, in which the legal, theological and ethical issues that stem from the text, as well as the historical framework in which it arose, are specific academic and personal concerns for me. Furthermore, the Qur'ān may be the basis for Islam as a faith, but its teachings are reflected in so many different ways in so many different cultures all professing the Islamic faith; this phenomenon is in itself a remarkable testimony to the way a sacred scripture permeates and goes beyond so many cultural, linguistic, geographic and historical boundaries.

As a book of faith, the Qur'ān has its own place in the hearts and minds of the believers as the eternal speech of God; but as a piece of literature, understood in the context of sacred literature, the text assumes many different life forms, and demands interpretation at various levels. It is working within all these different forms that makes reading any sacred text an intellectual challenge.

In the course of any form of religious dialogue, comparisons between the Bible and the Qur'ān can often be simplified and misleading. Both texts live in the literary traditions subsequent to revelation and both are reflected alongside different persons, Muhammad and Jesus. For me, the ultimate question is how to approach a sacred text on the premise that what is being approached may never really be fully grasped because of the limitations or parameters within which we work. Thus, the task for the believers is understanding and living a book that by its very nature will eternally remain partially elusive to humanity.

Muhammad Suheyl Umar

Here are a few reflections that surface from the recesses of my memory as I try to remember my relationship with the Qur'ān from my early childhood.

I was brought up in a household embedded in faith and permeated with the presence of the scripture. My childhood reminiscences tell me that the scripture was, above all, a sacrament for me, and I use the word with all its traditional Christian or Muslim connotations. It was only later that I learnt, in academic terms, the reason for that. It was due to the fact that the Qur'ān is regarded as the central theophany in Islam, and the idea of the Qur'ān as sacrament and theophany has been the fundamental and dominating idea of the Muslim mind. According to one of the most fundamental doctrines of Islam, the Qur'ān is the uncreated Word of God. This is to say that in the case of the last revelation God spoke to mankind in Arabic, and the Arabic language itself became the body of his Word. That is precisely the reason that in Islam one cannot talk about the 'incarnation' (that is, the 'enfleshment') of the word, but rather of the 'inlibration' (that is, the 'embookment') of the Word. The Word did not become flesh in Islam; it became book.

The Qur'ān as sacrament and theophany has a parallel in Christianity to the relation that the Virgin Mary carries to Christ. She was the recipient of the revelation (Christ), as Muhammad was the recipient of the revelation (the Qur'ān). For people who come from a Christian background, where the Gospel accounts of the life of Jesus play a major role in faith, it is well to keep in mind that Muhammad plays second fiddle to the Qur'ān. He is enormously important for Islamic religiosity, but his importance stems from his relationship to the Qur'ān.

This is how I entered into the universe of the Qur'ānic scripture in my early days. As I grew up other dimensions were added to it, namely learning its language and understanding its commandments. In the traditional Islamic context, education begins with memorization of the Qur'ān, which is the highest possible wisdom. That becomes a source of never-ending inspiration for me.

The presence of the Qur'ān as sacrament and theophany took the outward form of recitation. The Qur'ān is not read; it is recited, and a recited book is a book that is embodied within human beings. The sounds and rhythms of the recitation have a direct influence on the human body. Through reciting the Qur'ān, people come to embody the book and thereby, indirectly, to 'incarnate' the word.

Then the message of the Qur'ān started to enter into my psyche. I know through experience that the Qur'ān has a rational and intellectual dimension that can be grasped without recourse to the recited text itself. However, it is far from true that the whole of the Qur'ānic message can be grasped through study. Faith in Islam demands practice. The most fundamental of all Islamic practices, the ṣalāt, consists of cyclic movements and Qur'ānic recitation, all of which serve to embody the Qur'ān within the person who performs the prayer. To the extent Muslims live the reality of their religion, the Qur'ān becomes the reality of their minds, their hearts and their bodies.

I have experienced the Qur'ān in all these dimensions throughout my life with increasing degrees of perception, but above all the recitation of the Qur'ān has been, throughout life, my chief means of concentration upon God – which is itself the essence of my spiritual path and indeed of every spiritual path. My reading thus becomes the equivalent of a long drawn-out invocation of the name 'Allah'. Moreover, I am conscious that the Qur'ān is a flow and an ebb – that it flows to me from God and that its verses are miraculous signs (*āyāt*) which will take me back to God – and that is precisely why I read it.

Rowan Williams

From an early age, I was fascinated and absorbed by the stories of the Bible; growing up in a Presbyterian household in South Wales, I was not regarded as eccentric, since this was still a culture in which the words and names and narratives of the Bible were common coin. I have always been intrigued by the way in which the Welsh revivals led to the naming of rural Welsh communities with biblical names, just as the Nonconformist chapels nearly all had such designations (Bethel, Siloh, Seion, Moriah and so on). To live as a Christian was to live in the very landscape of the Bible.

If I had to describe my sense of the significance of scripture, this is still the kind of language I should use. We do not just read, we *inhabit* the Bible. We come to recognize its stories as the 'story of the soul' and of the community of souls that is the Church. This is the shape of life that God's presence creates, this is the rhythm and movement of our words and thoughts before God.

So as I read scripture, these are the main considerations for me. I read each day, morning and evening, in the context of the Office of the Church, and several times a week also during the celebration of the Eucharist; and I read for the purposes of preparing sermons, theological lectures, addresses for spiritual retreats, and so on. My aim in reading is not to find instructions but to open myself to 'God's world' – to the landscape of God's action and the rhythms of life lived in God's presence. That is why for me, as for so many, the Psalms have a special place as the voice of the heart touched by God – sometimes praising, sometimes grieving, sometimes angry and irrational, but always turned Godwards. And, like Christians throughout the ages, I try to read the Psalms as a way of uniting my prayer to that of the risen Jesus Christ, who is the centre of the scriptures and the touchstone of all interpretation.

I read most often in English now, but for years have read also regularly in Welsh; and for study have used Greek and Hebrew, which I love specially. To read in more than one tongue is for me an important part of sensing quite how large the landscape of God's work is.

The great Anglican commentator Bishop Westcott said in the nineteenth century that we need simply to 'gaze' on scripture until it begins to open out before us. That is what I believe must be done in reading: entering the new world.

Tim Winter

My experience of scripture has three primary focuses, which I hope are only superficially distinct.

First, my academic work, which in the past three or four years has increasingly focused on issues in Muslim–Christian relations. This seeks to be 'tradition-directed'. I take the consensual Sunni-Jama'i reading of the Qur'ānic and *ḥadīth* canon to be normative, with internal diversity a part of that normalcy. My interest lies in exploring the possibility of extending classical canons of scriptural exposition in order to engage with certain manners of contemporary thought. For instance, I am writing an article on the gendering of God in Muslim scriptures, putting Irigaray and Lacan into conversation with Ibn Arabi and the *kalām* authors. The idea is to propose that the 'word made word' is gender-neutral, and hence less marginalizing to any gender, than the traditional Christian ideas of the 'word made flesh' against which Irigaray argues. The subsequent problem relates to the role of (male) prophets as privileged mediators.

Linked to this in some ways is my exploration of the use of scriptural lexis by rival sects in the early Ottoman empire. The transformation of the Turkish literature by the embedding of Qur'ānic vocabulary was handled very differently by the *ulema* in comparison with the use made of it by rural sectaries.

A further area of my academic work is my work on the design of internet-mounted *ḥadīth* databases. This involves liaising between a team of twenty traditional scholars in Cairo, and the major institutions of Islamic studies in the West. Issues include the editing, conservation and digitizing of manuscripts (see www.ihsanetwork.org).

Secondly, I use scripture in a largely classical way in my mosque preaching. I deliver Friday sermons most weeks, in a variety of mosques in the UK and America. The Muslim sermon is very much an exercise in scriptural exposition, and the task is to provide the next link in an unbroken chain of expositors stretching back to the Prophet, which nonetheless speaks to the condition of an extremely diverse congregation.

Thirdly, scripture is the word of God, and is thus a kind of Real Presence. It is cultivated and cherished not only for its discursive content, but as a breath of the eternal: 'For those that believe, it is a guidance and a healing' – *Fuṣṣilat* (41) 44. I have had the privilege of studying the art of Qur'ānic cantillation at the Maʿhad al-Qirā'āt and other traditional institutions in Cairo. I have also been privileged to receive *ijāza* (traditional teaching authorization) from several masters of *ḥadīth* studies in Mecca and elsewhere. This is always conferred as a responsibility and a reminder that each generation is accountable for the preservation, proclamation and mediating of God's word. The holder of the word is thus partially akin to the priest who may touch the reserved sacrament. His response to scripture will shape his eternal fate.

Frances Young

Two contexts are most significant in my reading of scripture. Some tension between the two was once my experience, but there has been increasing integration over the years.

The primary experience has been reading scripture in church worship, and my first learning about scripture occurred in church-based Sunday schools. The presumption of such reading was, and remains, that scripture can be understood straightforwardly (or, as some would put it, 'literally'). Yet I was at a very early age aware of questions – about the account of creation in the book of Genesis, for example, or the so-called 'nature miracles' in the Gospels – the point being that they did not cohere with the scientific account of the universe.

Such questions and doubts were exacerbated by theological study at the University. Modern biblical criticism, which for some was an exercise in apologetics with respect to the incompatibility of the scriptures and modern knowledge, in fact challenged many of the assumptions with which I had grown up, despite being raised in a theologically 'liberal' tradition. The Bible was treated as a historical document, to be set in its original context, if its witness to God's saving events in history was to be properly understood. I learned the biblical languages, Hebrew and Greek. The different 'mind-set' of its authors compared with that of modern readers was to be taken into account in assessing the 'facts' behind the scriptural interpretations offered in the texts. I was educated in biblical criticism in the period when there was extreme scepticism as to whether the historian could be sure about the authenticity of any of the words and deeds of Jesus recorded in the Gospels.

I was also a Methodist lay preacher, interpreting scripture in the context of church worship, and for years I found I could not preach from the Gospels, given that one of my core values is integrity and I was intellectually uncertain about what I could and could not accept as 'fact'. This was the period of maximum tension between the two contexts.

Postmodern critical theory, coupled with immersion in the biblical interpretation of the Church Fathers (mainly the Greek, and to some extent the Latin and Syriac authors of the first four centuries of Christianity), has made it possible to reintegrate my reading and response to the scripture. Both alert one first to the metaphorical nature of language, particularly with regard to God, the being who transcends all thought and language (to treat language as 'literal' with respect to God is to reduce God to the limits of our creaturely understanding, while the Fathers acknowledge God's accommodation to our level in the language of scripture and the incarnation); secondly, to the impossibility of separating fact from interpretation and the need to be aware of the presuppositions of the interpreter as well as the text and author; thirdly, to the important interaction of reader-text-author for the meaning of the text 'now'; and fourthly, to the significance of the *future* of the text, and its potential to generate new meaning in new situations (as distinct from the 'archeological' approach of modernity which trapped the text in the past). As Ephraim Syrus put it in the fourth century, scripture is like a fountain, and one should not suppose that the single one of its riches that one has found is the only one to exist – it simply is not possible to drink the fountain dry.

Chapter 2

Listening to God, learning from scripture

The respective scriptures of Christians and Muslims alike are charged with revelatory power: attentiveness to these texts enables believers to discern the divine Word communicating with them. In this chapter, one Christian and two Muslims present their understanding of how this dynamic operates. Tom Wright expounds the story of Jesus' disciples on the road to Emmaus as paradigmatic for a Christian reading of the Bible. Vincent Cornell explores the theme of 'listening' in the context of the Qur'ān, while Tim Winter emphasizes the importance of a right spiritual disposition in approaching the scriptural text. Interspersed with these presentations are two dialogues built around pairs of passages from the Bible and the Qur'ān. The first relates the reading of the divine message in the written word to the discernment of that message in the signs of creation; the second looks at the theological concept of the 'Word of God' as that is scripturally presented in Christianity and in Islam.

On the road to Emmaus

Tom Wright

I wish to present a brief account of how, for Christians, the Bible is perceived and how it can function, through examining the remarkable story which occupies centre stage in the final chapter of Luke's Gospel. The story of the two disciples on the road to Emmaus (Luke 24.13-35) has been much loved, much studied, and had much written about it, and it offers an inexhaustible well of ideas and possibilities for many conversations. I shall focus on three ways of looking at the story: first, what Luke is saying about the scriptures of Israel; second, how Luke intends this story to function within the community that reads it, too, as scripture; and third, how this chapter can, does and might function for Christians today.

Luke and the scriptures of Israel

From the beginning of his Gospel, it is clear that Luke intends his story of Jesus to be seen as the continuation and climax of the Old

Testament's story of Israel. His opening scenes remind us of 1 Samuel: the conception and birth of John the Baptist and Jesus take us back to the conception and birth of Samuel and the call of David. Luke also locates his story within the wider world of the Roman empire and its middle-eastern satellite kingdoms. If this is how the story of Israel reaches its fulfilment, it must be time for the whole world to be confronted and challenged by Israel's God.

This way of understanding the framing of the gospel is confirmed at several subsequent points, notably by comments such as we find, only in Luke, at the Transfiguration scene: Moses and Elijah on the mountain were talking to Jesus 'about his *exodos* which he was to accomplish in Jerusalem'.[1] The two dominant prophetic figures of the scriptures, standing for Torah and Prophets, indicate to Jesus the way he must go, what lies ahead of him there, and what it will all mean. The Greek word '*exodos*' can mean both 'departure' and 'death'. In this context, it invests those two ideas with the further meaning, that what Jesus will accomplish in Jerusalem is the new Exodus, not now from the slavery of Egypt, but from a deeper and darker slavery still.

The people for whom he will accomplish it, as becomes clear at the end of Luke 24 and particularly in Acts, is not Israel only, but the wider world that was in view from the moment Caesar Augustus unwittingly precipitated the journey to Bethlehem. Just as Moses challenged the empire of Pharaoh, Elijah the Baal-worship of Ahab and Jezebel, and Isaiah the gods of Babylon, so the kingdom which Jesus announces must challenge the empire of Caesar and, behind that gain, the sovereignty of death.

Luke continues to hint that the story he is telling is bringing the scriptural narrative to its climax. His repeated *dei*, 'it is necessary',[2] indicates, as this chapter makes clear, that what happens to Jesus 'is necessary' because this is where the scriptures had pointed all along. Luke thus has Jesus invoke the scriptures of Israel to explain that the story he is telling is not free-standing, or detached from the longer purposes of the creator God. This was where it all had to end.

One of Luke's many reasons for doing this is that his point would have been shocking to any first-century Jew, including the disciples themselves. Among the many different first-century ways of reading Israel's scriptures, there were powerful traditions of storytelling, sometimes in competition with one another and sometimes in collaboration. Books as diverse as Jubilees, Ben Sirach and the Wisdom of Solomon offered strikingly different narratives, which went back to Abraham or even Adam and brought the story forward from the end of the explicitly biblical period, that is, not long after the Babylonian exile, into the time of the writers. The book of Daniel was read in the first century not least to ascertain the chronology of when God's Kingdom would arrive, as we see in Josephus and 4 Ezra. The Qumran sect, for its part, told its own story, in terms of reinterpreted prophecy, as the account of the real 'return from exile' which left them now waiting for the final dénouement. The revolutionary groups of the period (including the hard-line Pharisees) were sustained by similar speculation. Christianity came to birth in a world where its central claim – that the scriptures had been fulfilled in this way, rather than some other – was, precisely by belonging so obviously on the map of first-century Jewish thinking, in competition with several other incompatible readings. The clash in Acts between the Christians and the Jewish authorities is not about isolated dogmas, or about (dis)obedience to particular commands, but about the question: whose story is the true fulfilment of the scriptural narrative?

The story Luke tells is shocking in a second way. Unlike the other retellings and completions of Israel's narrative on offer in this period, it centred upon the death and resurrection of Israel's Messiah. Up to now, 'resurrection' had had two meanings within Judaism. First, it referred to the final resurrection of all the righteous, or even – in some texts – of righteous and wicked alike. By no means all Jews believed this, but those who did thought of an actual bodily resurrection at the end of 'the present age', ushering in 'the age to come'. Second, from Ezekiel 37 'resurrection' language could refer metaphorically to the restoration itself, seen as the real, final return from exile. 'Resurrection' was thus both metonymy and metaphor: one element within the great final restoration, and a figure of speech for that final event seen as God's rescue of his people from the ultimate enemy.

This explains the puzzlement of the two disciples on the road to Emmaus. They had hoped, and imagined, that Jesus would be the Messiah, the one through whom Israel would be liberated.[3] But they now assumed that his violent death at the hands of the Romans meant that 'redemption' had not yet occurred. What could be less like redemption than the execution of the King of the Jews at the hands of pagan rulers? Is that not precisely the depth of exile? The reports of an empty tomb, and of a vision of angels saying that Jesus was alive again, stirred no sense of recognition, no flicker of an underlying narrative at last coming true. What they are now offered is a new way of reading Israel's scriptures: new not because it was a narratival reading (that was already common coin), nor because this reading envisioned the story reaching its climax in the hearers' own day (that too was normal), but new in the sense that the story was now reaching its climax with the death and resurrection of Israel's Messiah. The birth of early Christian hermeneutics is traced by Luke to Jesus himself, to the risen Jesus as he explains to his two puzzled followers that this was where the story had been going all along:

> Foolish ones, said Jesus, how slow of heart you are to believe all that the prophets had said! Was it not necessary that the Messiah would suffer these things, and enter into his glory? And, beginning with Moses and all the prophets, he interpreted to them in all the scriptures the things concerning himself.[4]

Luke thus challenges the view, which has been very popular in many circles, that the early Christian understanding of the Old Testament focused on isolated proof texts – a verse from Daniel here, a passage from Isaiah there, a couple of Psalms for good measure. The 'necessity' of which Jesus speaks is not the necessity of 'fulfilling', in that random way, a certain number of key texts, but the necessity which comes from the inner coherence of the whole narrative. Jesus speaks of that which was common to many first-century narrative readings of Israel's scripture: the sense that Israel's story was presently stuck in the mode of exile, because of the sins of the people, but that when God acted to forgive Israel's sins, and to end this exile, this great event would at last fulfil the longer purpose for which Israel was called in the first place, namely that through it God would bring blessing, justice and peace to the world.

As soon as we understand the story in this way, many major parts of Israel's narrative come into focus: from the call of Abraham, through the birth and near-sacrifice of Isaac, through the Joseph story and the sojourn in Egypt, the Exodus and conquest, the monarchy and its prophetic critique, and – finally and crucially – the exile, which (as in Daniel 9) clearly had not been undone by the geographical 'return', but was continuing as long as the pagans were ruling over Israel. At every stage the story speaks of God's surprising call of his people to undergo suffering, slavery, judgement and exile, and of God's equally surprising rescue of them through and after such trials. How better might this story reach its divinely ordained goal than with Israel's ultimate representative, the Messiah himself, undergoing shameful death, the very deepest point of exile, and emerging triumphant in new bodily life? This, Luke is telling us, is what Jesus explained to the two on the road, and then to the others in the upper room.[5] Jesus' death and resurrection are like that of Isaac, only more so; like the Exodus from Egypt, only more so; like the return from exile, except that they are the reality to which the unsatisfactory geographical 'return' had pointed forward. This is where the story was meant to end up.

In 24.44-7 Luke has Jesus go further. Now that the story has reached its appropriate, if startling, climax, it must be implemented in the way the prophets had imagined. Once Israel's exile is undone, the whole world must be brought within the new creation of justice and peace. 'Repentance and forgiveness of sins are to be announced to all nations, beginning from Jerusalem.'[6] This is not to be understood merely as the proclamation that individuals should repent and so find forgiveness, but that – again, as the prophets had foretold – 'repentance' as a new possibility, and 'forgiveness' as a new fact about God and the world should be announced as realities in which the nations were summoned to partake. The story thus points forward to Acts, in which, still very much to their own surprise, the disciples find themselves as the agents of God, in the power of the Spirit of Jesus, announcing within Caesar's kingdom that there is 'another king',[7] and declaring that through this newly enthroned lord of the world a new way of life has opened up for all peoples, a way in which repentance and forgiveness are the keynotes, a way through which the nations may be healed. Our own recognition of the many ways in which the church has failed to live up to this calling should not prevent us from seeing its inner logic.

Luke's story is thus designed to show how the scriptures of Israel have come to their climax in Jesus, and that they now shape the mission of the church in the world. This leads to the natural question: how then does Luke intend his own writings to function within the same emerging church?

Luke's story and the Church's life

It has long been fashionable to say that the writers of the New Testament did not know that they were writing 'scripture'. However, clearly anybody who writes a book like Luke's Gospel has set themselves the task of constructing a narrative that links to, and in one sense intends to complete, the narrative of the Old Testament scriptures, and which does so with the intention of providing a formative, grounding narrative for the early Christian community. This may not correspond exactly to later ideas of 'scripture', but it means that Luke was doing much more than merely compiling a story about Jesus out of historical or cultural curiosity.

In particular, Luke's story is designed to ground the early Christian community not simply in the story itself but in the events to which it refers – in this case, obviously, the events of Jesus himself, his life, death and resurrection. Here we run into a different scholarly fashion, or rather the combination of at least four: (1) the long-standing assumption in some quarters that early Christian faith looked on to the Second Coming rather than back to the events concerning Jesus; (2) the conviction, particularly among the Lutheran and existentialist theologians of the Bultmann school, that to look back to historical events was to falsify Christian faith and risk turning it into a 'work'; (3) the supporting assumption that the Gospels do not in fact convey much historical information about Jesus himself; and (4) the postmodern insistence on the difficulty of moving from a text to an extra-textual reality – even of moving to some kind of authorial intention. I have argued against all of these elsewhere.[8] My point for mentioning them here has to do with the different place that the Bible holds in Christianity to that held (in so far as I understand it) by the Qur'ān within Islam.

Luke intends his book to function as part of the foundation charter of the church. But his point is that God's saving deed occurred, not in the writing or reading of this book and others like it, but in the events concerning Jesus himself. However high a valuation Christians place on the Bible in general and the New Testament in particular, the Bible is not the centre of God's revelation or the main object of faith. That place belongs to Jesus himself. All authority, says Matthew's Jesus, has been given to him[9] – not to the books which speak of him, vital though they are.

Speaking of Jesus himself in this way has been thought problematic from various theological, literary and cultural points of view. People have often suggested that, because the Gospels reflect the faith of the early Church and the theology and rhetoric of the evangelists, they cannot also be taken to refer directly to actual historical events concerning Jesus. I remain convinced that this is simply a sophisticated version of the problem of the hare and the tortoise: we all know that the hare does indeed overtake the tortoise, and in the same way we should recognize that the Gospels do indeed refer to Jesus himself. We will not understand Luke unless we recognize that he is not simply reflecting the faith of his community, or expressing his own, but is speaking of Jesus himself as the one in whom God's plan of salvation came to completion. Luke knows the difference between parable and history, and he intends his basic story to be the latter. He has carefully located his account of Jesus within the larger story of Israel, and part of the point of Israel's story was always that the redeemer God and the creator God are one and the same. A redemption which occurred somewhere other than in the real, created world would not be the redemption for which Israel was longing. Granted that redemption and salvation are redefined in the New Testament around Jesus himself, this redefinition does not consist (except for the gnostics) in moving away from history into an ahistorical sphere of private spirituality. For Luke, telling the story of Jesus makes the sense it does because these things really happened. Scripture thus matters for the Christian in the same way that water-pipes matter to a householder: they make available a source of life that comes from somewhere else. The pipes must be connected to an external supply, or they will be useless. For the Christian, in the first century or the twenty-first, Jesus himself is the water supply.

The first purpose of Luke's story as part of Christian scripture is thus to point back continually to the foundation events, the extra-textual historical reality concerning Jesus. But Luke, like all the evangelists, of course does far more than that; indeed Luke 24, and especially the story of the road to Emmaus, is a classic example of what Christians have discovered scripture to be. Precisely because the Jesus of whom the stories speak is both the Jesus who lived, died and rose in the first century and the living Lord of the world and the church, stories whose primary meaning has to do with things that happened in the first century also carry the power to evoke his presence in subsequent times. Here a Christian understanding of the New Testament as scripture badly needs to move beyond the sterile 'either/or' of much post-Enlightenment criticism (either history or faith, and so on) and embrace not just a 'both-and' theology – for saying 'both-and' can simply reinscribe the difference between the two elements thus brought side by side – but a new way of articulating the reality which includes but transcends both.

In particular, there are signs that Luke intends the Emmaus Road story to function in this way for subsequent readers. Without in any way downgrading our insistence that Luke means to describe things which actually happened, it is easy to see that the story is told in such a way as to dovetail with what we know, from elsewhere in Luke's writing, was taken to be the shaping and defining life of the early Christian community. In Acts 24.2, Luke highlights four elements: the apostles' teaching and fellowship, the breaking of bread, and the prayers. In the present passage, the teaching and bread-breaking are central, and the dynamic between them is rich and subtle. In Luke 24.30, Jesus takes the bread, blesses it, breaks it and gives it to them – the fourfold action recalling, of course, the Last Supper and similar occasions elsewhere in Jesus' ministry. When, having done this, the risen Jesus disappears from view, the first reaction of the astonished disciples is to say: 'Did not our hearts burn within us as he talked to us on the road, as he opened the scriptures to us?' They rush back to Jerusalem, and tell the other, in Luke's matchless description, 'what had happened on the road, and how he had been made known to them in the breaking of the bread'.[10]

Luke has told the story in such a way as to invite his readers into the same experience, generating fresh enactments of the same sequence of events. As the disciples on the road heard Jesus expounding the scripture, so those who read this book will find their hearts burning within them in turn, and thus be invited to the bread-breaking in which they will find his presence with them still. Luke's Emmaus Road story can thus serve as a paradigm not only for a Christian understanding of the Old Testament, in the way outlined in the first part of this essay, but also for a Christian understanding of the New Testament. The New Testament is the story of Jesus and his followers, told in such a way as to generate and sustain the continuing historical community that seeks to know and follow him in turn.

This is emphasized and explicated further in the final paragraphs of the book. Luke wants his readers to understand their own life and vocation as the continuation and implementation of that fulfilment of Moses and the prophets which occurred in Jesus' death and resurrection. His book is designed to constitute its faithful readers as the people through whom this is to happen, and to equip them for the task. The book is not, of course, their only equipment. Just as the gospel story points beyond itself to Jesus himself, so the scriptural commissioning of the disciples points beyond itself to the promised Holy Spirit,[11] through whom they will be enabled to play their allotted role within the unfolding narrative. But the book, Luke-seen-as-scripture, gives direction, focus and meaning to the energetic life which the Spirit will provide. In Luke's final scene, the readers are invited not only to observe the first disciples in joyful worship but to join them.

Luke 24 thus alerts us to various features of how the New Testament seems designed to function as scripture in the Christian sense, in addition to its articulation of a Christian understanding of the Old Testament. It tells the story of Jesus, a story whose primary meaning is contained in the fact that it happened in the real world, the world the creator God made and has now begun to remake. But it tells this story in such a way as to generate and sustain the ongoing community of

Jesus' followers, to help them in their own searching of the scriptures, to bring their bread-breaking into Jesus-shaped focus, to point them to their Spirit-led tasks of announcing repentance and forgiveness. The New Testament sketches out the eschatological drama within which being a Christian makes the sense it does. It tells the ongoing story within which Christian worship, mission, belief and behaviour find their meaning. To read this story is to be drawn towards, or deeper into, the events concerning Jesus, and the events in which his Spirit is still at work.

Luke 24 and Christian ways of reading scripture

Finally, I will use Luke 24 as an example of some different ways in which Christians read and use scripture now. These can be divided up many ways: formal and informal, public and private, 'academic' and 'devotional', large-scale and small-scale, and so on. These divisions in turn interact with various 'senses of scripture' which have themselves been catalogued and studied extensively. I choose three examples designed to cross over these various boundaries.

First, there is public reading of scripture within liturgy. Most Christians in mainstream churches, whether or not they make a habit of personal scripture reading and study, encounter scripture in public reading during church services. Within Orthodox, Roman Catholic and Anglican churches, the reading of a Gospel passage forms a key element in the eucharistic liturgy, where it gains precisely the meaning made explicit in Luke 24.32-5: scripture is designed to set the heart on fire, and so to prepare us to recognize the Lord in the breaking of bread.

But Luke 24 also points to a quieter, perhaps less obvious meaning of the public reading of scripture, seen in the ancient monastic offices and preserved in the daily services around which classic Anglican devotion has centred, Mattins and Evensong.[12] These offices provide a framework for readings from Old and New Testaments, characteristically between ten and thirty verses long depending on the content, frequently following a lectionary. The point of the readings is not primarily to inform or teach the content of the specific readings, though those who live within this framework know how often they seem remarkably appropriate. The point is rather to proclaim and celebrate the story of God and the world, focused on the story of God and Israel and thence on the story of Jesus as the one who made, and makes, the living God present, and in whom Israel's history was summed up. Luke 24, in its insistence on Jesus as the fulfilment of scripture and of the Church's life as the fresh development of the same story, suggests exactly this kind of appropriation of scripture. The two readings serve not as isolated, detached snippets of didactic material, but as small windows through which the enormous narrative from Genesis to Revelation can be viewed as a whole. Each service thus becomes a celebration of the entire story, fulfilling the biblical command to declare God's mighty acts, to his glory.

Likewise, the readings constitute the community as the people who, through hearing in faith, are drawn into the story and shaped by it. That is why, in morning and evening prayer, the readings are preceded by the Psalms, followed by biblical songs of praise, and lead into the Creed and the prayers. This public reading of scripture invites, among other things, the further kinds of reading to which I now turn.

Second, there is the historical study of scripture. Though many different 'senses of scripture' have been distinguished, exegetes from early times to the present have insisted on the importance, and usually the priority, of the literal sense, which frequently means the historical sense. The post-Enlightenment period developed the art of detailed 'historical criticism', and the so-called 'historical-critical method', sometimes explicitly intending thereby to call traditional Christian faith into question. This has been so successful that many Christians now perceive historical study of scripture to be hostile towards, and destructive of, authentic and orthodox faith and life. My own conviction, however, is that authentic Christianity cannot evade the challenge of history, and that the risks involved belong with the risks taken by God himself in becoming incarnate – indeed, in making a world in the first place, and in calling Israel. I cherish the advice of the great biblical scholar Sir Edwyn Hoskyns: 'Bury yourself in a dictionary and come up in the presence of God.'[13] I have frequently found, and I have seen others find as well, that the microscopic study of words and meanings, of contexts and genres, of authors and emphases, generates fresh awareness of the greatness of God, the accomplishment of Jesus, and the power of the Spirit.

This can be illustrated by one small point from Luke 24 itself. Luke says of the two disciples, observing Jesus break the bread, that 'the eyes of them both were opened, and they recognized him'.[14] Luke uses almost exactly the same Greek words as those found where Adam and Eve ate the forbidden fruit, and 'their eyes were opened, and they knew that they were naked'.[15] Luke is hinting that with Jesus' resurrection the curse of the Fall has been undone: sin and death have been overcome, and the narrative of the new creation can now proceed with the project of the original creation, which had been put on hold because of human idolatry and rebellion.

Alongside public reading and historical study, and complementary to both, is a third, more devotional reading, known in many traditions – not least, the Ignatian. The Emmaus Road story is often used as a classic example of the latter. The reader is invited, in prayer and contemplation, to imagine the narrative and to enter into it like an actor in a play.[16] Reading the story, we become one of the two disciples, whether the talkative Cleopas or his silent companion. Within their tale of puzzlement and complaint, poured out at Jesus' invitation, we are able to articulate our own puzzlement, disappointment, fear and grief. We cannot predict how the conversation will continue. At some point in our prayerful imagining, Jesus himself may begin to speak to us, reminding us of the biblical story, inviting us to see our complaints from a new angle, from (dare we say) God's point of view. At some point we may find ourselves recognizing him in a new way – in the Eucharist, in the faces of the poor, in the very events which had seemed so tragic and frustrating. And at some point we may find ourselves freshly energized to speak of what we have seen and heard, and may find our vocation given new focus and impetus.

Obviously, this kind of reading works more naturally with some parts of scripture than with others. Working out what the equivalent would be when faced with a chapter of Paul would be interesting. But this, or something like it, is how millions of Christians approach scripture day by day, and draw from it the strength that comes from having been with Jesus.

Public reading, historical study, and private meditation are three very different, but in my view complementary, ways in which scripture is encountered within Christianity. There are many more – not least, group study, which can combine all three. Luke 24 is itself only one starting-point among many, one small window on a much larger world. Yet I hope that I have shown how it is possible to see here some of the characteristic features of a Christian understanding of scripture. I trust that this will help Christians and Muslims together to establish a context within which we can understand one another's traditions, and explore their parallels and divergences, with sensitivity and appreciation.

Listening to God through the Qur'ān

Vincent Cornell

> Say: It has been revealed unto me that a group of the Jinn listened [to the word of God] and said, 'Verily we have heard a marvellous Qur'ān' (*innā sami'nā qur'ānan 'ajaban*). [al-Jinn (72) 1]

> Verily those who listen respond [to God] (*innamā yastajību alladhīna yasma'ūna*). [al-An'ām (6) 36]

'Listen, may God have mercy on you' (*anṣitū, raḥimakum Allāh*). Every Friday, in every mosque that follows the Mālikī school of law from North Africa to the Arabian Peninsula, this admonition is recited just before the start of the midday sermon (*khuṭba*). Although the 'listening' mentioned here refers specifically to the words of the sermon, the sermon itself is preceded by a group recitation of the Qur'ān that begins a little over an hour before the prayer, building to a crescendo of voices that fills the mosque and the neighbouring streets as the time for prayer approaches. In the ritual world of Mālikī practice, the Friday prayer is all about what language specialists call 'active listening'. In the great mosques of major towns and cities, one both recites and listens to the words of the Qur'ān; one listens again to the verses and invocations of the *qāri'* (reciter), who also calls worshippers to listen to the sermon; one listens attentively to the sermon, which is itself a commentary on the words of God and the teachings of the Prophet Muhammad; and one listens and responds to God's speech as recited in the prayer. One is also reminded in the prayer that 'active listening' is reciprocal; in every cycle of prostration the worshipper repeats, 'God listens to the one who praises Him' (*sami'a allāhu li-man ḥamidahu*). In few other contexts is it so clear that 'those who listen respond', whether it is the worshipper or God Himself.

The concept of listening is a major theme of the Qur'ān, and the Arabic root 'he listened' (*sami'a*) is a major focus-word of the Qur'ānic text. In the Qur'ānic view of salvation history, God 'speaks' and human beings 'listen'. The response of Muslims to God's command is, 'We hear (or listen) and obey' (*sami'nā wa aṭa'nā*);[17] those who actively listen to God and obey his commands prosper and are saved.[18] Believers are enjoined not to be like those who say, 'we hear' but do not listen.[19] As in the Friday prayer, Muslims are encouraged to 'listen to God's verses when they are recited'; but one should not then 'become arrogant, as if he had not heard them'.[20] In the Qur'ān, the ear that listens to the word of God is described as the outward counterpart to the heart, which 'sees' or intuits divine truths; when the ear becomes deaf to the word of God, the heart becomes 'blind' to the vision of the truth.[21] Finally, from the perspective of the history of religions, tradition 'speaks' and people 'listen'. Sometimes, tradition speaks the same message as that of the Qur'ān: 'They said, "Oh our people! We have heard (listened to) a scripture revealed after that of Moses, confirming what was in it, and guiding unto the truth and the direct way."'[22] But at other times, the voice of tradition speaks a different message from that of God, as when the people of Egypt said to Moses, 'This is no more than concocted magic. We have never heard of this from our ancestors.'[23]

A writer on Islam once remarked that if Jesus represents for Christians the divine word incarnate, then the Qur'ān represents for Muslims the divine word 'inlibrate'. Although there is truth to this statement, since it is the Qur'ān and not the Prophet Muhammad that is the theophany of Islam, it is somewhat misleading in that it ignores the sense in which the Qur'ān, more than 1400 years after its revelation, still constitutes a living voice for Muslims. Although the Qur'ān was compiled as a book, and refers to itself as such numerous times, the concept of 'book' conjures up, in the popular imagination, a passive image of musty tomes consulted by bearded scholars who maintain the 'dead hand' of inherited tradition. The current climate of Islamic traditionalism and fundamentalism fostered by some Shi'ite religious elites and the partisans of Neo-Ḥanalī Islam, represented by the Wahhābīs of Saudi Arabia and by Taliban and Jamaati activists in Pakistan, reinforce this image. In such a context, the Glorious Book that is the Qur'ān represents, in the words of the Egyptian-American scholar Khaled Abou El Fadl, the *authoritarian* as much, if not more, than the *authoritative*.[24]

I would argue, along with Abou El Fadl, that while the Qur'ān is fundamentally authoritative for all Muslims, the 'voice' that it asks humanity to listen to actively is not the voice of authoritarianism. The word *'qur'ān'* means both 'reading' and 'recital'. As a verbal noun (*maṣdar*) of the form *'fu'lān'*, it carries the connotation of a 'continuous reading' or 'eternal lection' that is recited and 'listened to' over and over again. Even the word *kitāb*, which the Qur'ān also uses to describe itself, does not only connote 'book'. In medieval Arabic, *kitāb* stood in a more general sense for any type of transmitted communication, whether it was written or verbal. The Qur'ān, as *kitāb Allāh,* is thus more than an ordinary book. In a well-known passage, the Qur'ān calls itself *umm al-kitāb* – 'Mother of the Book', or paradigm of divine communication.[25] Since it embodies the word of God,[26] not only the meaning of the Qur'ān, but also the words and even the individual letters of its text are suffused with divinity and mystery. Rituals associated with the divine word in Islamic practice range from the requirement that one must make an ablution before picking up and reading a copy of the Qur'ān to the use of words and phrases of the Qur'ān in regional forms of magic and divination. In pre-modern times the 'voice' of the Qur'ān even ventured into the occult, and its esoteric wisdom (ḥikma) remains a fundamental part of Sufi hermeneutics. The Spanish Sufi Ibn 'Arabī (d. 1240) arranged the entirety of his magnum opus al-Futūḥāt al-Makkiyya ('Meccan Inspirations') according to the arrangement of the verses of the Qur'ān when read from back to front.[27]

The Qur'ān 'speaks' to the Muslim in many ways, irrespective of whether it is read as a book, heard as a recitation, used as an inspiration for art, manipulated as a form of magic, or interpreted as a source of divine wisdom. When interpreting the Qur'ān, nothing is more absurd than to approach it in the manner of a religious fundamentalist, and to claim in an authoritarian manner that one may read the text in only one way, or that each verse contains only its literal meaning. A famous verse deals with the problem of over-interpretation by dividing the message of the Qur'ān into two parts.[28] The muḥkamāt or verses of legal import (another meaning of 'Mother of the Book') are accessible to all; they provide the rules and guidance that all Muslims must follow when integrating the teachings of the Qur'ān into their daily lives. Other verses, however, are ambiguous (mutashābihāt) and should be interpreted only by those who are deeply versed in knowledge. This, the Qur'ān implies, is the specific domain of theologians and philosophers. Verses such as these should not be subjected to baseless speculation. Instead, they are to be interpreted through a hermeneutical process that the Qur'ān calls ta'wīl, a type of interpretation that historically included rational, contextual, linguistic, philosophical, and even mystical approaches to the meaning of the text.

Muslim fundamentalists who are threatened by multiple varieties of interpretation have unwittingly become like those the Qur'ān chastises for 'hearing but not listening'. It is not that they have strayed from Islam itself; rather, they do a grave disservice to their fellow believers by limiting the sources of divine wisdom. They also do a disservice to the word of God by rendering it univocal. A god that speaks in only one interpretative language can never be the god of a universal religion. Like a boulder blocking the source of a stream, the authoritarian approach to Islam leaves Muslims thirsty for knowledge in a parched and barren field of religious and moral obligations, when in reality there is more than enough sustenance in God's speech to nourish many gardens and orchards of ideas. Indeed, given the deep symbolism of the concept of 'verse' in the Qur'ān, how can it be otherwise? The Qur'ānic term for 'verse' is *āya*. This word or one of its variants is employed nearly four hundred times in the text. Most frequently, *āya* refers to evidences in the world of nature that demonstrate the existence of God. Sometimes, the term may refer to a miracle confirming the truth of a prophet's message, a revealed message in general, or even a fundamental point in a particular discourse. Because of its multivalency, the best English translation of *āya* is 'sign'. Ibn Manẓūr (d. 1311–12), one of the most authoritative lexicographers of pre-modern Islam, also agreed in his dictionary *Lisān al-'Arab* (The Tongue of the Arabs), that 'sign' (Arabic *'alāma*) is the best synonym for *āya*.

In theological terms, an *āya* of the Qur'ān is best characterized as 'a statement in the speech of God'. The totality of these statements in the Qur'ān constitutes the divine message as revealed to the Prophet Muhammad. But each statement of the Qur'ān is also a 'remembrance' or a 'recollection' (*dhikr* or *dhikrā*),[29] which, when listened to actively, awakens human beings to discern the existence of God through his creation. Thus, each *āya* of the Qur'ān is a sign in a symbolic or semiotic sense that points to another level of understanding which, in turn, reaffirms the message of revelation. The Muslim who develops a sense of the sacred by listening actively to the speech of God must thus learn two different 'languages' at the same time – the Arabic language of the Qur'ān and the 'language' of nature, which also expresses the speech of God. God created the world as a book. His revelations descended to Earth and were compiled into books. Therefore, the human being must learn to 'read' the world as a book. This aspect of spiritual intellection is exemplified in the Qur'ān by the prophet Abraham, who discerned the One God out of the multiplicity of heavenly phenomena, and the prophet Solomon, who was inspired to learn the 'discourse of the birds'.[31]

The Book of the World to which the Qur'ān points constitutes the non-linguistic form of God's communication with humanity. The phenomena of nature are 'words' that form the 'sentences' that make up the *āyāt* ('signs') in which God's speech is expressed. Each natural phenomenon that makes up a 'word' of God's non-linguistic speech is thus a symbolic marker or signpost (*'ālam*, pl. *'alāmāt*) – what semiologist Charles Sanders Peirce called an 'index' – that points the person of spiritual intelligence toward the Ultimate Reality (*al-Ḥaqq*).[32] In listening to God by 'reading' the world, reason (*'aql*) and inspiration (*ilhām*) work together to enable the believer to decipher God's non-linguistic speech. As noted previously, this is expressed in the Qur'ān through the metaphor of the 'linking' or intuition of the heart. Such Qur'ānic passages also form the scriptural bases for the Sufi conception of the 'Way of the Heart' that is a hallmark of Islamic mysticism. Not only in Sufi texts, but also in the discourse of the Qur'ān itself, the Book of the World is seen as a macrocosmic Qur'ān, to which the written Qur'ān points. The same idea of a macrocosmic scripture is also expressed in the Qur'ān by the concept of the 'Preserved Tablet' (al-lawḥ al-maḥfūẓ),[33] an idea which parallels the Jewish concept of an eternal, pre-existent Torah as the source of God's law. In Islamic theology, the related metaphors of the Preserved Tablet and the Book of the World gave birth to ideas as diverse as the Mu'tazilite concept of the 'created Qur'ān' and the mystical-philosophical notion of theurgy. This esoteric doctrine, which was derived from a type of Greek esotericism known as *semeia*, posited sympathetic correspondences between the Preserved Tablet, the Book of the World, and the Qur'ān, and formed the theoretical basis of alchemical and divinatory texts such as the tenth-century 'Picatrix' (Arabic *Ghāyat al-Ḥakīm*).

But the *āyāt* of the Qur'ān do not only constitute signs. They are also verses. And as such, they represent the linguistic aspect of communication between God and the human being. This linguistic communication, which is fundamental to the three great Middle Eastern religions of Judaism, Christianity and Islam, is based on the belief that the ultimate guarantee of the truth of religious experience lies in the fact that God revealed himself to human beings. In Judaism and Islam, God did not manifest himself in a visible form, as he did in Christianity. Instead, he 'spoke' to his prophets in a humanly understandable language. This concept of direct, linguistic communication is central to the Islamic concept of revelation and is fundamental to the idea of the sacredness of the Qur'ān. In a way that corresponds in part to the system of semantics developed by the French linguist Ferdinand de Saussure, revelation contains the 'speech' (*parole*) of God, which is expressed in a living human language or 'tongue' (*langue*, Arabic *lisān*).[34] 'If any of the polytheists comes to you seeking your protection, keep him close to you so that he may hear the speech of God (*kalām allāh*)', says God to the Prophet Muhammad.[35] As for the nature of this speech, 'We have made it a Qur'ān in Arabic, so that you may understand.'[36]

But God did not 'speak' to the Prophet Muhammad in a direct, one-to-one manner. According to the tenets of Islamic theology, which stresses absolute transcendence (*tanzīh*) over immanence (*tashbīh*), this would be impossible.

40

Two beings of utterly different and incompatible natures and powers cannot speak 'man-to-man'. Instead, divine-human communication is effected through revelation, which in Arabic is known as *waḥy*. In pre-Islamic usage, *waḥy* was used to connote communication in general, particularly that which was mysterious, secret, or private, such as when animals communicate with each other through their sounds. In modern parlance, the phrase *awḥā ilayhi* could mean 'he communicated to him', or 'he signified to him'.

Thus, the term *waḥy*, which denotes revelation, shares with the term *āya*, which stands for the semantic content of revelation, a sense of secrecy or esotericism. In societies such as that of seventh-century Arabia, which had only recently developed an alphabet and was just beginning to emerge into literacy, letter-magic is a common form of divination. It is no surprise, therefore, to find that all of the terms used to describe revelation in the Qur'ān, including its linguistic and written expressions, contain an air of mystery and hint at esoteric knowledge. In the Qur'ān, the birth of language is described as an esoteric revelation, for God told Adam to reveal his wisdom by conveying to the angels 'the names of all things'.[37] *Anbi'hum*, the phrase used to describe Adam's conveyance of language to the angels, comes from the Arabic root *naba'a*, which literally means 'he made known', or 'he prophesied'.

Because of the ontological distance between God and the human being, most revelatory experiences must be mediated, just as electricity in high-tension power lines must go through a 'step-down' process at a substation before it can be used in homes. The unmediated presence of God can kill. This is expressed in the Qur'ān in the story of Moses, where God reveals himself to a mountain and it is destroyed.[38]

> The mediator or 'transformer' that transposes divine revelation into a human form of communication is variously described in the Qur'ān as the angel Gabriel, the Holy Spirit (*al-rūḥ al-qudus*),[39] or the Trustworthy Spirit (*al-rūḥ al-amīn*).[40] But sometimes the Qur'ān and the traditions of the Prophet Muhammad also allude to a direct experience of revelation. The descriptions of such experiences indicate a profound transformation of the Prophet's inward self; so profound in fact that it is accompanied by intense suffering, physical pain, and the feeling of being choked. The Prophet is reported to have sweated on cold days, his face darkened, he fell into a faint, and at times he groaned when the voice of God came to him. But as one would expect, the divine speech

did not come to him in the form of a human voice. In a famous passage that is found in *Ṣaḥīḥ al-Bukhārī*, the Prophet reported: 'Sometimes [revelation] comes to me like the ringing of a bell (*salsalat al-jaras*); this is the most painful manner of revelation to me; then it departs from me and I have understood from the sound what [God] meant to say'.[41] This is not just a historical account. It reminds the believer, in a very profound way, that actively listening to God is not easy. In the words of the Tunisian historian, sociologist, and jurist Ibn Khaldūn (d. 1406), the pain of which the Prophet spoke is a result of the fact that the human soul is by nature unprepared for such a supernatural experience. In effect, says Ibn Khaldūn, the Prophet was forced through such experiences to exchange his humanity for a more profound state of 'angelicality'.[42]

Contemporary Muslims are not expected to undergo such profound changes as did the Prophet Muhammad. But in listening to the word of God we are supposed to take the Prophet's example as a guide for our own behaviour. This example not only includes the rules and regulations found in the Qur'ān and the traditions of the Sunna. It also includes accounts of more inward, and even esoteric experiences, such as those described above. In the early sixteenth century the Moroccan Sufi 'Abdallāh al-Ghazwānī (d. 1529) used the metaphor of the bell, described by the Prophet in his account of the experience of revelation, to describe the 'pealing' or reverberation of God's word in the heart of each believer. For the most accomplished Muslim, listening to the word of God goes beyond the outward observance of the written word of the Qur'ān and includes listening to the melody of the divine harmonic that is the subtext of the Book of the World.[43]

Three centuries before al-Ghazwānī the same message was expressed by the Egyptian Sufi Aḥmad al-Būnī (d. 1225), the author of the still popular work of theurgy, *Shams al-Maʿārif al-Kubrā* ('Sun of the Greatest Forms of Knowledge'). Although Būnī has been criticized by Muslim exotericists as far back as Ibn Taymiyya (d. 1328), and contemporary scholars are forbidden to consult manuscripts of his works at the Egyptian National Library, his words about listening to the 'bell' – the speech of God as it appears in the human heart and the Book of the World – are particularly important for Muslims today, whose spiritual world is arguably more impoverished than it was in the Middle Ages: 'The bell tolls for each person. He who listens to it is elevated and is taken from the world for union with God, which, in fact, is the goal of prayer.'[44]

Scripture dialogue I: Signs of God

Psalm 19; al-Rūm (30) 19-30

Christians and Muslims receive the Bible and the Qur'ān respectively as conveying to them in some sense the word of God. Yet both scriptures also – as the two passages considered here show – speak of other 'signs' of God which are to be found in the created order, and which in some sense complement those delivered through the written word. How do these two dimensions of divine communication – what in medieval Christian tradition are called two 'books of God'[45] – mutually interpret one another? What is required of the human respondent to read the signs aright, and how are misreadings to be accounted for by either faith? These are questions with which both Christians and Muslims have wrestled over the centuries.

In the setting of a dialogue of scriptures, there is also the challenge of accepting the semiotic reality of the other's universe of meanings, and relating that to the ways in which our own community discerns the language of God. While there are some helpful pointers in our shared past to exploration of these issues in the dimension of 'natural theology', our engagement brought into a new and sharp focus the 'cross-reading' of the Qur'ān by Christians and of the Bible by Muslims. If this is a venture to be pursued with a seriousness of respect and integrity in the future, there needs to be the development of a hermeneutic of trust which will involve reappraisal of many of our attitudes.

Biblical text: Psalm 19

[1]The heavens are telling the glory of God;
    and the firmament proclaims his handiwork.
[2]Day to day pours forth speech,
    and night to night declares knowledge.
[3]There is no speech, nor are there words;
    their voice is not heard;
[4]yet their voice goes out through all the earth,

and their words to the end of the world.
In the heavens he has set a tent for the sun,
>   5which comes out like a bridegroom from his wedding
>   canopy,
>   and like a strong man runs its course with joy.
6Its rising is from the end of the heavens,
>   and its circuit to the end of them;
>   and nothing is hid from its heat.
7The law of the Lord is perfect,
>   reviving the soul;
the decrees of the Lord are sure,
>   making wise the simple;
8the precepts of the Lord are right,
>   rejoicing the heart;
the commandment of the Lord is clear,
>   enlightening the eyes;
9the fear of the Lord is pure,
>   enduring forever;
the ordinances of the Lord are true
>   and righteous altogether.
10More to be desired are they than gold,
>   even much fine gold;
sweeter also than honey,
>   and drippings of the honeycomb.
11Moreover by them is your servant warned;
>   in keeping them there is great reward.
12But who can detect their errors?
>   Clear me from hidden faults.
13Keep back your servant also from the insolent;
>   do not let them have dominion over me.
>   Then I shall be blameless,
>   and innocent of great transgression.
14Let the words of my mouth and the meditation of my
heart be acceptable to you,
>   O Lord, my rock and my redeemer.

Notes on Psalm 19

1. 'God' is *ēl* (used also of a Canaanite deity), as opposed to *Yhwh* ('Lord') in 7-14.
9. Some scholars emend 'fear' to 'word'. The sequence of words 'law' [*tōrah* – more accurately, 'teaching'] – 'decrees' – 'precepts' – 'commandment' – ['word'] – 'ordinances' may be taken as roughly equivalent to one another, rather than precisely distinguished; the psalm's tightly controlled rhythms in this section build up a climactic sense of the perfection and desirability of the *tōrah*.
10. 'Desired' is expressive of an intense emotion – 'coveted'.

Commentary on Psalm 19

The psalm celebrates the Word of God in three contexts: in the natural creation, in the written word of scripture, and in the appropriation of the word in the hearts of God's servants. The stylistic break between the sections dealing with the first two of these is so marked that most scholars have concluded that verses 7-14 have been added to provide a counterbalancing emphasis on the Mosaic *tōrah* to an earlier hymn in praise of the cosmic glory of God. Whatever the textual history, though, the psalm in its present form teaches that the signs of the divine are to be found both in the natural and the revealed order. In medieval Christian thought, this principle was expressed in terms of two books of divinity: 'Besides that written one of God, another of His servant Nature, that universal and public manuscript, that lies expansed unto the eyes of all: those that never saw him in the one, have discovered him in the other.'[46]

How are these two 'books' to be read? The psalm first presents the ordered sequence of created phenomena as a visual language speaking directly of the Creator.[47] There is no suggestion here of a special insight needed to grasp this message; it is immediately accessible to all the world. This sense of a truth manifestly obvious underlies the subsequent Jewish polemic against idolatry, involving as that does the substitution of a creature for the Creator. This polemic is in turn taken up by Paul, for whom therefore 'natural theology' becomes the basis of divine judgement.[48]

In the case of the word revealed in the Mosaic law, the issues of discernment are more complex. On one hand, the scriptural message itself is without ambiguity: it is 'perfect', 'sure', 'right', 'clear', 'pure', 'true'. However, the reader, and would-be follower, of this message is at the same time conscious of the 'errors' and 'hidden faults' which impede a full and obedient reception of the word. The problem here may be thought of originally in terms of inadvertent transgressions of the law; in other texts in the psalms, though, there is recognition of a dimension of interiority in our failure to respond to God,[49] and this is deepened in the Pauline consciousness of the reality and power of sin within the human psyche.

Qur'ānic text: al-Rūm (30) 19-30

[19]He brings the living out of the dead and the dead out of the living. He gives life to the earth after death, and you will be brought out in the same way. [20]One of His signs is the way he created you from dust and, lo and behold! you became humans, scattered far and wide. [21]Another of His signs is the way He created spouses of your own kind for you to find repose with one another – He ordained love and kindness between you. There truly are signs in this for those who reflect. [22]Another of His signs is the creation of the heavens and earth, the diversity of your languages and colours. There truly are signs in this for those who know. [23]Another of His signs is your sleep by night and by day and your seeking some of His bounty. There truly are signs in this for those who can hear. [24]Among His signs, too, are that He shows you the lightning that terrifies and inspires hope; that he sends water down from the sky to restore the earth to life after death. There truly are signs in this for those who use their reason. [25]Among His signs too are that the heavens and the earth stand firm by His command. In the end, you will all emerge when He calls you from the earth. [26]Everyone in the heavens and earth belongs to Him, and all are obedient to Him. [27]He is the One who originates creation and will do it again – this is even easier for Him. He is above all comparison in the heavens and earth; He is the Almighty, the All Wise.

[28]He gives you this example, drawn from your own lives: do you make your slaves full partners with an equal share in what We have given you? Do you fear them as you fear each other? This is how We make Our messages clear to those who use their reason. [29]And still the polytheists follow their own desires without any knowledge. Who can guide those God leaves to stray, who have no one to help them? [30]So (Prophet) as a man of pure faith, stand firm in your devotion to the religion. This is the natural disposition God instilled in mankind – there is no altering God's creation – and the right religion, though most people do not realize it.

Notes on al-Rūm (30) 19-30

20-25. The word *āya*, 'sign', is used both of natural phenomena, as here, and of the verses of the Qur'ān. It can also indicate any miracle or startling event which displays divine power.

23. As in other verses in this sequence of 'signs', a complementary pair is here pointed out – in this case, rest and activity.

25. The second part of the verse complements the shaking of the earth on the Day of Judgement (when 'you will all emerge when He calls you from the earth') with its present stability; both point to the power of the Creator.

28. The example of the human hierarchy of slavery, in which the 'superior' shares none of his wealth with the 'inferior', is used as a parable to point out the impossibility of setting any creature in association with the Creator.

30. The 'natural disposition' or *fiṭra* is the innate recognition of monotheism which is the natural state of human beings, and which comes to its fullness in the religion of Islam.

Commentary on al-Rūm (30) 19-30

This *sūra* of the Qur'ān brings together signs from the natural and the human world to point to the unique and surpassing power of God. The title *al-Rūm*, 'the Romans', refers to the prophecy at the start of the chapter that, despite their apparently hopeless state, the Byzantine ('Roman') armies would defeat the forces of Persia.[50] This extraordinary outcome would be according to the purposes of God, who thereby shows his power to bring 'the living out of the dead'. The theme of this startling divine power is then pursued through a series of signs in which the human and the natural both feature, and in which complementary pairs are coordinated to express the transcendence of the Creator over all created distinctions.

The use of the word '*āya*', common to both created phenomena and the revealed word, shows how all things can serve to demonstrate the majesty and the uniqueness of God. In order to read these divine messages correctly, the passage speaks variously of the human faculties of 'reflection', 'knowledge', 'hearing' and 'reflection'. These are not to be sharply distinguished one from another; they are all expressions of the natural recognition of the truth of monotheism which in Islamic belief is innate to human beings – and which provides the basis for the correct response of obedient submission which all are invited to make. The Qur'ān in these verses argues persuasively on the basis of experiences which are accessible to all to establish the evidence of this natural theology, which scripture thus confirms.

Nevertheless, the last verses also acknowledge the undeniable obduracy of much – even the majority – of humanity in refusing to acknowledge this luminous truth. The Qur'ānic analysis of such an attitude is to characterize it as a wilful 'ignorance' which is culpable on the part of those who display it. There is indeed the suggestion that this is the result of a 'leaving to stray' initiated by God, but this is not developed in such a way as to excuse the ignorant, nor does it complicate the simple remedy that the Qur'ān prescribes: namely to acknowledge the natural and evident truth to which humans are repeatedly summoned back by the prophetic message. There is no humanly insurpassable barrier of sin to be overcome here; in this sense, Islamic anthropology can be described as basically optimistic.

Reflection 1: Divine consistency and surprise

Both passages acclaim a God who reveals himself through natural and human phenomena as well as through scriptural texts – indeed, both seek to coordinate these different witnesses to the divine self-manifestation. A distinction can indeed be drawn between the two 'books' of nature and scripture, but this can relate only to the modalities through which the knowledge of God is communicated and apprehended. Neither Islam nor Christianity can accept the notion that there is any inconsistency between natural and confessional theology, even if in Christian faith the latter has generally been thought to excel the former in its richness and depth. This is a direct consequence of the consistency (or faithfulness) of God, who is equally the author of both theological volumes. For the faithful reader, the two are mutually interpretative: scripture opens up the depth of the world in which we are set, while that God-spoken world in turn is the context in which we read the revealed text.

Both Muslims and Christians have had to reflect on the way in which the divine authorship of both 'books' is to be understood. In the case of scripture, orthodox Sunni Muslims have held to the principle that the Qur'ānic text in its entirety is the direct, infallible Word of God that has existed from all eternity.[51] Christian theories of the inspiration of scripture have been more varied, but most would want to reject a view of the Bible which divided it up into some parts which were 'divine' as against others which were merely 'human'. On the other hand, the idea of consistency itself suggests that scripture must in some sense generate ways in which the more difficult passages are interpreted by the more straightforward. In the case of natural phenomena and historical events, the situation is equally complex. Do calamitous and destructive events, for example – such as an earthquake leading to a major loss of life – form part of the pattern of signs through which God speaks to humanity? At different periods of both Muslim and Christian history, there have been those who would want to affirm this, perhaps interpreting such an event as a sign of divine punishment or warning; but this itself raises major ethical problems about the character of a God who would act in such a way.

However, a concern for consistency does not mean that divine conduct is to be judged, and divine signs deciphered, solely in terms of existing conventional morality and expectations. On the contrary, both scriptures witness to a God whose purposes are displayed in counter-intuitive and startling ways. This is apparent in the way that the Qur'ān coordinates contrasting pairs of phenomena as pointers to the divine, in the subversive character of many of the Gospel parables, and – above all – in the emphasis in both faiths on God as one who enacts the greatest sign, of resurrection, the bringing into new life of that which is dead.

Reflection 2: Human readings and misreadings

While Christians and Muslims assert the intelligibility and transparency of scripture and nature as media through which the one God communicates himself, they also both recognize that to read these written and phenomenal signs requires of humans certain dispositions or qualities – attentiveness, understanding, wisdom. Both also then have to reckon with the distressing fact that large numbers of human beings seem in fact to be impervious to the message – unable to grasp the import of the signs, and resistant to implementing their injunctions. This contrast between the inherent perspicuity of the word and the persisting obduracy of its hearers poses a significant challenge within both faiths, but the way in which the problem is addressed differs significantly between the two, according to whether it is characterized as 'sin' or 'ignorance'.

The problems become still more complex when either religious community takes into account the readings of the divine signs made by the other. In the realm of 'natural theology', it has been possible to see a remarkable degree of convergence between Christians and Muslims. Even in the crusading period, when the two communities were locked in to mutual hostility and suspicion, a sense of collegiality could develop across religious boundaries – there were to be found scholars on both sides 'more inclined to examine the arguments of thinkers than their faith, trusting in the image of the creator in us all to search out traces of the divine handiwork'.[52] A generous appreciation of the right discernment of God on the part of the other at this time was undoubtedly facilitated by a shared reliance on the insights of the Greek philosophical heritage.

In relation to the scriptural discernment of God, in contrast, there has often been a refusal of the other's ability to read correctly the divine message. On one hand, Christians have found it difficult to accept that the Qur'ān, as a message received later than the fullness of God's self-communication in Jesus Christ, can be counted as truly divine revelation. On the other hand, Muslims have viewed Christian readings of the Bible under the heading of *taḥrīf*. Generally translated 'alteration', this is a concept which can operate at different levels: instability of the received text through the existence of variant forms; misguided interpretations of the scriptural message; or, the most serious, deliberate alteration of the original teachings to promote falsehood. In both directions, openness to the scriptural texts of the other as those texts are actually received and read in the community of faith poses sharp challenges to Christians' and Muslims' own readings. It may be that the wider horizons of discerning together God's signs in the natural order and in human history can help to promote mutually healing readings of one another's holy texts, and so build up a hermeneutic of trust.

Readings of the 'Reading'

Tim Winter

It is generally accepted among Muslims that our communication skills currently leave much to be desired. We are called by our scriptures to be a kerygmatic people, to continue the Prophetic 'arise and warn'; ours, too, is a 'great commission'. Yet we are, by and large, not understood. I wish to propose the idea that scriptural interpretation, far from being a recondite game for insiders, might serve as a hugely important instrument in dispelling some widespread misapprehensions about our community. As an Arab proverb points out: *al-insānu ʿaduww mā jahil* – 'man is the enemy of what he does not understand'.[53]

Islam proposes that scripture is a theophany – in fact, nobody would dispute that the Qur'ān is *the* great theophany of the religion. Some have even proposed that Islam holds a doctrine of what Harry Wolfson called 'inlibration' – that is to say, that whereas in Christianity the Word is made flesh, in Islam the Word becomes book.[54] Hence, we are told, the apparent parallelism between some of our formative sectarian troubles: the Muʿtazilites were the Arians of Islam, because they denied the pre-

50

existent nature of the Word. As with all such ambitious parallelisms, however, this one soon proves treacherous. The 'Word made book' really refers to *kalām*, not to *kalima*: to speech, not to word. There certainly is no idea that this theophany is a divine hypostasis.

Nonetheless, those unfamiliar with the internal spiritual metabolism of Muslim piety must not assume that the text is just a text, to be read as are other texts. Neither is the Qur'ān simply 'the best of texts' (39.23). It is not an inlibration of God, but it is still an authentic presence – a Real Presence, if you like. Just as mainstream Christianity experiences God during the Eucharist, so too an almost equivalent moment is experienced in Islam when Muslims open their scripture. The Word resonates within us; we breathe, as it were, the breath of God Himself, and we are transformed. Hence the verses of the text are *āyāt*, 'signs', which point to heaven not only cognitively but – as it were – iconically. As Toshihiko Izutsu has shown, the flagship Islamic argument for God is located in the capacity of the inmost nature of human beings, what the Qur'ān terms the *lubb*, 'seed' or 'core', truly to intuit the existence of the supernatural worlds. We gain this through contemplating the *āyāt*, the signs that are in nature – the *vestigia Dei*, if you like. But we are also guided, and saved, by allowing the mysterious otherness of the scripture to reshape and to heal our souls.[55]

A few lines from a short story by the Hyderabad writer Hasan Askari. These concern a poor, illiterate Indian woman. Despite her inability to understand the text, or even to read it, she experiences it as the central theophany in her world:

> She would then spread the prayer-mat, a beautiful soft Persian piece, its direction towards the East. She was now going towards the corner in the room where wrapped in green silk lay the Qur'ān. She would take out the Qur'ān and hold it to her heart. Her eyes then were full of tears. She was holding a book which she loved and respected so much and yet she was unable to read. She would then recall, crying like a child, that moment when the Voice repeatedly said to the Prophet in the cave of Hera: Read, Read in the Name of the Lord. And the Prophet had said in utter helplessness: I cannot read.
>
> Then she would return to the prayer-mat, lifting the Qur'ān above her head, saying as though: O Book! You are above my understanding. My head is nothing more than a place whereupon you rest.
>
> Having sat down not occupying the entire prayer-mat but a part of it, for to occupy the whole of the prayer-mat was to her

an act of arrogance, she would open the book knowing only to keep the right side up, and to begin where she had left the previous day.

For a long time she would allow her eyes to rest on the two open pages before her. The letters in green ink from right to left, row beneath row, each shape mysteriously captivating, each dot below or above a letter an epitome of the entire scripture, each assembly of letters a group of dervishes raising their heads in zikr, each gap between two enigmatic shapes a leap from this world to the next, and each ending the advent of the Day of Resurrection.

She would thus see a thousand images in the procession of that script and would move from vision to vision.

After spending much time in just looking at the open book, she would then, with strange light glowing on her face, lift her right hand and with the right finger start touching the letters of each line, then another line, to the end of the page. What transpired between the book and that touch, and what knowledge passed, without any mediation of conscious thought, directly into her soul, only the Qur'ān and that strange reciter could know. The entire world stood still at this amazing recital without words, without meaning, without knowledge. With that touch a unity was established between her and the Qur'ān. At that moment she had passed into a state of total identity with the word of God. Her inability to read the scripture was her ability to hear once again: Read! Read, in the Name of thy Lord.[56]

In this way, scripture is a healing. The Qur'ān itself insists on this: 'And we reveal of the Qur'ān that which is a healing, and a mercy to those that have faith' (17.82). The word *shifā*', 'healing', regularly connotes the Qur'ānic experience throughout our literature. It indicates a sense of ease, of presence, of repair. Elsewhere in the text honey is praised as having the same qualities: 'From their bellies comes a drink of diverse colours, in which there is a healing for people' (16.69). The recital of the Qur'ān, the experience of this breath of God mysteriously resonating within one's breast, is akin to the sweetness and the healing properties of honey.

The Prophet, upon whom be peace, was – as 'Ā'isha remarked – 'the virtues of the Qur'ān'.[57] Contemplating him, we experience the majesty and the beauty of the Book. There is a *mysterium tremendum et fascinans* in his *sīra* or life story. He himself, the text's mysterious vessel, experienced it as a healing, as well as a terrifying disclosure of the divine power and infinitude. So he is told: 'We have not revealed the Qur'ān to you that you might be grieved' (20.2). As exemplar of the transformative power of the text, the Prophet is a vision of a human being who can be restored to Adamic perfection, as God's *khalīfa*, viceregent on earth. The Names of God which are disclosed in the scripture are, *mutatis mutandis*, his as well. God is the Merciful, the Prophet is merciful. God is the Judge, the Prophet is judge, and so on. He remains entirely human, not divine, but he has become fully theomorphic. As Imām al-Būṣīrī (d.1296) put it:

> Leave aside the claims which the Christians make for their prophet, but speak what praise you will in his regard,
> For the most that can be known is that he is mortal man, and that he is the best of God's creation in its entirety.[58]

Those unfamiliar with our tradition are often unaware of this aspect of Prophetic devotion – that it is through contemplating the Prophet that we are transformed by the Qur'ān, and that he himself is its deepest and most irresistible commentary. He himself became *al-Shāfī*, 'the healer', not only in his healing miracles but also in his ability to form a visible presence of the healing that God offers through the Qur'ān.[59]

Only when we have grasped this will we begin to understand the centrality of the Qur'ān, and of the practice of its formal cantillation, in Muslim prophetology and soteriology. Jalāl al-Dīn Rūmī has, according to the *Christian Science Monitor*, become the best-selling poet in America,[60] yet Coleman Barks and his other New Age mediators have detached Rūmī from his life-support system, which is Prophetic and Qur'ānic. As Rūmī himself sings:

> I am the Qur'ān's slave so long as I draw breath.
> I am dust on the path of Muhammad, the chosen one.[61]

Elsewhere, in a rare Arabic moment, Rūmī praises the Blessed Prophet as follows: 'Here is my beloved; here is my physician; here is my teacher; here is my cure.'[62]

To give one brief example from the Turkish world – the eighteenth-century saint Ibrāhīm Ḥaqqī writes:

> In this base world, faithlessness and strife
> conspire together thwarting true joy in life.
> Our Lord's beloved, O chosen one, give us help
> on the last day.[63]

The reference here, of course, is to the orthodox Muslim yearning for the Prophet's intercession at the resurrection.

The question this naturally raises, however, is the following. We can hope that those not of our religious family can intuit, perhaps through analogies with comparable structures in their own traditions, the way in which Qur'ānic interpretation is Prophetic, and is a road to salvation. As I mentioned earlier, we Muslims have generally been rather bad at explaining the centrality of the Qur'ān and the Prophet as sacred presences in our lives. But the question today must be: is this meditative style of intuitive exegesis likely to produce a healing between religions, rather than, as the texts seem to suggest, among Muslim believers alone?

It must be admitted that there is a truculent temper among many Muslims today, triggered no doubt by the bewildering experience of being forced to live as subjects of a materialist modernity in whose direction we play no part. This temper – a consequence of, as well as a reaction against, the corrosive acids of modernity – impels us to read the Qur'ān in a new and intransigent way. Scripture, we must remember, is powerful but also immensely vulnerable. It has been placed in our hands with the assurance that there will be a general pneumatic guidance given to the community which will prevent its complete distortion. Nonetheless, it is probably fair to observe that nowhere has human ingenuity been more destructively abused than in the realm of scriptural interpretation. The *ḥadīth* is frank about this: 'Whoever interprets the Qur'ān according to his own private interpretation should prepare himself for hell'.[64] There is much evidence to suggest that the Islamic scriptural argument against the Biblical texts is not so much that they have been physically distorted as that they have been exegetically abused. Islam traditionally warns itself against succumbing to a comparable fate.[65]

Without a *magisterium*, Islam, as an intensely scripture-focused tradition, is nonetheless in danger of such abuse. Today, the canons of hermeneutic method, once firmly in the hands of slowly-evolving communities of ulema and muftis, have been democratized, and one immediate consequence of this is the calamity of extremism. A religion that recognizes the periodic need for just war, and which is currently experiencing difficulties in identifying to everybody's satisfaction the right custodians of the exegetic tradition, may get itself, and the world, into trouble. (There are analogous worries within the world of religious Zionism.)

Yet there is a control, and the control is spiritual. The Qur'ān proclaims that it is rightly received by those who are transformed by it rightly – that is to say, those who experience it as a healing, and who bring healing to the world. While I have little sympathy with the methods or implications of the pluralist theology of John Hick, I suspect that we need to take him seriously when he proposes a performative argument for the assessment of religions: are they hagiologically fertile? Paul Knitter, and a small community of Muslim thinkers influenced by him, have added the further question: are they liberative of communities?

What I am proposing, then, is that with the decline of classical, often very ancient, Muslim institutions and canons of scriptural management, and in a world in which many Muslims have every reason to be angry, an apparently new criterion for working with scriptures be evolved. The Qur'ān, traditionally understood, is rightly experienced as a healing to individual reading communities. Healing is, whatever the philosophers may now say, a trans-historical, universal human possibility. Once we establish this as the great purpose and gift of the Islamic revelation, further interpretation will be guided by the spirit, not the ego, and we will not – as the Qur'ān puts it – 'sell the signs of God for a paltry price' (3.199).

Scripture dialogue II: Word of God

Āl 'Imrān (3) 1-7; John 1.1-18

Both Muslims and Christians understand themselves to be addressed by a God who causes his Word to enter into the world in which they live, and the Qur'ān and the Bible in different ways hold that Word before their readers. In both faiths, moreover, while there is a clear focal point for that entry – the revelation of the Qur'ān to the Prophet Muhammad, and the life, death and resurrection of Jesus Christ respectively – there is also a history of revelation within which that decisive point is properly located and which provides a God-given context for its interpretation.

In both faiths, therefore, the very structure of the divine dispensation towards humanity requires that scripture should give its own reading of scripture. In addition to the historical or 'vertical' dimension of self-exegesis, the requirements of the hermeneutical process also generate a 'horizontal' dynamic, according to which certain parts of the text provide the interpretative key for approaching other parts. The opening verses of the third *sūra* of the Qur'ān, Āl 'Imrān (3) 1-7 and the 'prologue' to the Fourth Gospel, John 1.1-18, are two highly significant passages which illustrate these interlocking themes well; they also highlight deep divergences in the ways that the two faiths understand the Word of God theologically, and in the ways that they approach their respective scriptures.

Qur'ānic text: Āl 'Imrān (3) 1-7

¹*Alif Lām Mīm*

²God: there is no god but He, the Ever Living, the Ever Watchful. ³Step by step, He has sent the Scripture down to you (Prophet) with the truth, confirming what went before; He had sent down the Torah and the Gospel as a guide for people: ⁴He has sent down the distinction (between right and wrong). Those who deny God's revelations will suffer a severe torment: God is almighty and capable of retribution. ⁵Nothing on earth or in heaven is hidden from God: ⁶it is He who shapes you all in the womb as He pleases. There is no God but Him, the Mighty, the Wise: ⁷it is He who has sent this Scripture down to you (Prophet). Some of its verses are definite in meaning – these are the cornerstone of the Scripture – and others are ambiguous. The perverse at heart eagerly pursue the ambiguities in their attempt to make trouble and to pinpoint a specific meaning – only God knows the true meaning – while those firmly grounded in knowledge say, 'We believe in it all: it is all from our Lord' – only those with real perception will take heed.

Notes on Āl 'Imrān (3) 1-7

1. Twenty-nine of the sūras of the Qur'ān begin in this way with a letter or sequence of letters – six with this particular combination. Their significance has been much debated by Muslims. Some have sought to discern a hidden meaning or a mystic symbolism in them; others have seen them as 'ambiguities' understood only by God (cf. second note on 7 below).

3. The 'distinction' (*furqān*) has been variously understood. Some commentators identify it with the Law and Gospel, indicating that these revealed scriptures themselves already provide humanity with divine guidance; others see it as the Psalms, while yet others understand it to be a name for the Qur'ān. In any case, 'the Scripture' (the Qur'ān) confirms the divinely revealed texts which precede it.

Islamic theology has traditionally disputed the identity of the two scriptures certainly mentioned in this verse – *tawrāt* and *injīl* – with the actual books of the Law (*tōrah*) and Gospel (*evangelion*) accepted by contemporary Jews and Christians respectively, maintaining that the latter in particular has been severely altered, either deliberately or inadvertently, in the course of ecclesiastical history.

7. This verse distinguishes two different kinds of verses in the Qur'ān – the 'definite in meaning' (*muḥkam*) and the 'ambiguous' (*mutashābih*). The precise

import of both terms is not entirely clear, but what is apparent is that the former verses have more directness of meaning, and that they are to provide the basis for interpretation of the latter.

A further complication is provided by the possibility of two different systems of punctuation of the verse, rendered in differing patterns of Qur'ānic recitation. In the reading adopted by the translation, it is only Allah who can know the meaning of the *mutashābih* verses. If the pause after 'God' is suppressed, however, such knowledge also becomes more widely available 'to God and those who are firmly grounded in knowledge'.

Commentary on Āl 'Imrān (3) 1-7

The title of this *sūra*, 'the people of 'Imrān' indicates its themes. 'Imrān is in the Qur'ān the father of Moses,[66] and the primary teaching of the *sūra* concerns the relation of the Muslim community, and their revealed book, to those communities who before them have received a written scripture – the Torah delivered through Moses and the Gospel through Jesus. These opening verses strongly assert the Qur'ān's rightful place within this prophetic history, as the confirmation and completion of that which has been given as guidance by God before. In practical terms, the requirement that God's Word should be consistently truthful in its revelations has meant that Muslims cannot accept passages or interpretations of the Jewish and Christian scriptures which appear to contradict Qur'ānic teaching; the earlier revealed scriptures referred to here cannot therefore be simply equated with the holy texts as currently received in the Jewish and Christian communities. Indeed, according to some interpreters, an example of just such a divergence is provided in the opening verse of this *sūra*, where the insistence that 'there is no god save Allah' can be read as an implicit rebuke to the Christian doctrine of the divinity of Jesus as Son and Word.

While the first verses thus address the question of the consistency of the divine communication across different scriptures, verse 7 raises issues of the Qur'ān's own interpretation of itself. The meaning of the two kinds of verses distinguished here, the way they are to be related to one another, and the extent to which human beings have access to the meaning of the second category have all been contested issues within Islamic exegesis.[67] Two points, however, seem to be clear. First, this passage gives a warning against over-interpretation of particular verses and the fragmentation of the Qur'ānic text; conversely, it points within the scriptural revelation to certain points of reference as offering a clear and direct interpretation of the whole. Secondly, despite this, there is no suggestion that the *mutashābih* verses should in any sense be thought of as 'less' the Word of God than the others; they share equally in divine authorship, and are therefore imbued with divinely intended meaning – the basis for their singling out is the limited extent to which access can be had to that meaning.

Biblical text: John 1.1-18

¹In the beginning was the Word, and the Word was with God, and the Word was God. ²He was in the beginning with God. ³All things came into being through him, and without him not one thing came into being. What has come into being ⁴in him was life, and the life was the light of all people. ⁵The light shines in the darkness, and the darkness did not overcome it.

⁶There was a man sent from God, whose name was John. ⁷He came as a witness to testify to the light, so that all might believe through him. ⁸He himself was not the light, but he came to testify to the light. ⁹The true light, which enlightens everyone, was coming into the world.

¹⁰He was in the world, and the world came into being through him; yet the world did not know him. ¹¹He came to what was his own, and his own people did not accept him. ¹²But to all who received him, who believed in his name, he gave power to become children of God, ¹³who were born, not of blood or of the will of the flesh or of the will of man, but of God.

¹⁴And the Word became flesh and lived among us, and we have seen his glory, the glory as of a father's only son, full of grace and truth. ¹⁵(John testified to him and cried out, 'This was he of whom I said, "'He who comes after me ranks ahead of me because he was before me.'"') ¹⁶From his fullness we have all received, grace upon grace. ¹⁷The law indeed was given through Moses; grace and truth came through Jesus Christ. ¹⁸No one has ever seen God. It is God the only Son, who is close to the Father's heart, who has made him known.

Notes on John 1.1-18

1. The opening phrase recalls the creation story 'in the beginning' of Genesis 1 – the primordial opposition of 'light v darkness' is likewise taken up in verses 4-5.

1-2. The preposition 'with' (*pros*) used to position the Word's relationship to God has been more fully glossed by some as 'turned towards'.

6-8. This introduction of the figure of John the Baptist seems to be an excursus to the basic sequence of the passage telling of the Word (cf. verse 15).

9. This verse could also be read as: 'He was the true light that enlightens everyone coming into the world.'

13. The verse provides an explanatory amplification of the meaning of the expression 'children of God'.

14. 'Flesh' (*sarx*) indicates a human person, but highlighting particularly the dimension of vulnerability and mortality.

The expression 'lived [*eskēnōsen*] among us' literally implies the 'pitching of a tent [*skēnē*]', alluding to the way in which the divine presence (*shekinah*) was believed to dwell in the 'tabernacle' in the heart of the people of Israel. Cf. Sirach 24.8, where Wisdom is depicted as saying: 'Then the Creator of all things gave me a command, and my Creator chose the place for my tent [*skēnē*]. He said, "Make your dwelling [*kataskēnoō*] in Jacob, and in Israel receive your inheritance ".'

The generic reading 'a father's only son' given in this translation is an alternative to the more specific 'the Father's only Son'. From this point on, 'Word' language drops out of the Fourth Gospel, to be replaced by the imagery of sonship.

15. A second, parenthetical, note referring to John the Baptist.

Commentary on John 1.1-18

This prologue – doubtless one of the best-known passages of all Christian scripture – announces themes which will echo throughout this Gospel's account of Jesus' mission, and at the same time sets them in the long perspective of God's communication with his world, from its creation onwards. While the theme of the 'Word' certainly has, and probably is designed to have, resonances in the Greek philosophical tradition, its primary reference is certainly to the Hebrew religious world. The later patristic understanding of the Word as addressing Israel through the prophets, though not explicitly spelled out here, is present in germ. Reviewing and summarizing the interaction of God and his people as one of approach and indwelling, from some meeting rejection and from others acceptance, the evangelist speaks of the Word as a light which conveys both life and judgement. In Christian history, different readings of verse 9 in particular have been aligned with a difference in understanding the way this light addresses human beings: are we to see here the arrival into the world of a standard of judgement and challenge confronting us from beyond, or is the reference rather to an inner enlightening which is the heritage of all who are born into the world?

The pivotal point of the passage is the declaration in verse 14 of the Word's 'incarnation' – that is, his full realization as a vulnerable and mortal man. A few verses later, Jesus Christ is himself named for the first time, and from this point onwards the Fourth Gospel leaves the symbol of 'word' to speak rather in the emphatically anthropomorphic imagery of a father's son. Even before this turning point, though, the Word of God (*logos*) is described in the prologue using the personal categories of masculine, rather than neuter, grammatical gender forms. While later Christian theologians were to explain that the language of sonship should not be misinterpreted in the literalist terms of a physical generation, they also insisted on the irreducibility of this personalist dimension. It was then, from exploring the interpersonal implications of the Word's relationship of being 'turned towards' the Father that the dynamic of Trinitarian thought grew.

Reflection 1: God and his Word

Central to the very possibility of authentic faith for both Muslims and Christians is the conviction that the God who addresses and engages them in revelation is One who is faithful, consistent and true to Himself and to His creation. This has led them to insist on the eternity (in the double sense of pre-existence before creation and the continuation of existence without end)[68] of the Word of God, as a guarantee of the unswerving nature of the divine purpose, and also on that Word's indivisible unity with the divine being, as expressions of the authentic and immediate way in which God communicates. It is indeed interesting to note that both communities were disturbed in their first few centuries by major theological disputes over just these questions of the Word's status and eternity.[69] Behind these sometimes arid disputations, it is important to remember that what was ultimately at stake was the issue of God's faithfulness: can the divine will, spoken in the divine word, be trusted to act consistently for the good of creatures, rather than to be the arbitrary, fickle, or cruel product of a remote, capricious, or tyrannical character?

Nevertheless, despite these similarities in the underlying questions faced by Muslims and Christians, and the structural parallels in the kind of answers they have given, our faiths are divided over the locus in which the fullest statement of the Word of God to the world is to be found. Put simply, for Muslims this is the written text of a book, the Qur'ān, while for Christians it is the lived life of a human being, Jesus of Nazareth.

To highlight this point, the term 'inlibration' ('embookment') is sometimes used by way of comparison with the concept of 'incarnation'.[70] This distinction clearly has major consequences for an understanding of 'scripture' and its place within the community of faith, but it also underlies the difference in the way that the 'God-ward' status of the Word is understood in the two faiths. A contemporary Muslim scholar has memorably remarked of the biblical passage that 'John tells us that the Word was with God, but where we differ is with John's next statement, that the Word is God . . . no one has asserted that the Qur'ān is God.'[71] In this sense, the option for 'incarnation' or for 'inlibration' can be seen also as an option for or against a Trinitarian understanding of the one God.

Reflection 2: The Word and the words

The distinction between 'incarnation' and 'inlibration' also means that Muslims and Christians will approach in different ways the question of how the scriptural text serves to convey the Word of God. Orthodox Islamic belief accepts the Qur'ān as scripture because it itself constitutes the divine word as delivered directly to Muhammad in his capacity as a prophet – in this respect it differs even from the 'holy sayings' (*ḥadīth qudsī*)' in which God addresses Muhammad as a servant of God, and also of course from the rest of the Sunna of the Prophet, built around *ḥadīth* recording his deeds and words. While Islamic scholars have over the centuries built up a corpus of techniques to sift, compare and grade the *ḥadīth*, a sense of the immediacy and totality of the presence of the divine Word in the scripture has led to strong resistance to the application of historical-critical methods to the Qur'ān. On the other hand, some of the newer techniques of scriptural studies, taking as their starting point the literary structures of the text as given, provide perhaps more fruitful opportunities for biblical and Qur'ānic scholars to recognize shared areas of concern and approach.

The situation with regard to the Christian scriptures is more diverse. There is within the contemporary churches a very wide spectrum of views about the status of the biblical texts in relation to the Word of God – and, corresponding to this, a very wide variety of methods and approaches in interpreting the scriptures and applying their insights. Any Christian theology of inspiration, though, will have to recognize at the outset that the Bible is built up of very different elements. Within the New Testament alone, there are the sayings of Jesus, narratives of his life and of the apostles, practical and theological writings designed for the guidance of the early church, and the startling visions of the apocalypse. Moreover, both Testaments together show a constant process of reinterpretation of earlier passages of scripture in the light of later ones. The Christian consensus is certainly that the canon of the scriptures was in some sense recognized by the Church in acknowledgement of its inherent authority and authenticity rather than being defined purely as the result of an ecclesiastical process: that is to say, Christians have these biblical documents because they are the ones God wanted them to have. However, this does not translate convincingly for all Christians into a simple equation of the Bible with the Word of God. Many would want to say that if that Word is supremely expressed in the human person of Jesus, then the Word's presence will rather lie behind the scripted texts and be witnessed to by them.

Chapter 3

Legacies of the past, challenges of the present

Both the Qur'ān and the Bible are texts which reach out through time. In one direction, they set God's revelation against a horizon of historical depth which looks back to a series of divinely appointed human figures revered in common, though in different ways, by Muslims and Christians as well as by Jews. This chapter begins with scriptural passages relating to Abraham, one of the most important of these figures. Essays by Mona Siddiqui and Esther Mombo move the debate forwards in time, asking how a hermeneutic can be developed to derive contemporary guidance on contested issues from scriptures delivered into a different historical context. Both writers focus their attention on the question of woman's role within the community. This particular theme is then further explored in the concluding dialogue, based on a pair of passages, from the Qur'ān and the Bible respectively.

Scripture dialogue III: Abraham, a righteous man

Romans 4; al-Baqara (2) 124-36

Abraham stands out in both Christian and Muslim scriptures as a righteous man who is accepted by God, a recipient of divine blessing and a channel of divine mercy to the world. For Christians, the scriptural image of Abraham is bifocal. In the first place, there are the traditions recorded of the patriarch in the Hebrew scriptures, particularly the narrative cycles of Genesis 12–25. These then provided material for New Testament reflection on the significance of Abraham in the light of faith in Jesus Christ. Paul's midrashic treatment of Genesis 15 in Romans 4 seems to have been developed in a contested dialogue with contemporary Jewish accounts of a similar kind,[1] addressing the question of the rightful inheritors of Abraham's blessing. Within the Islamic understanding of scripture, by contrast, the figure of Abraham (*Ibrāhīm*) is caught up within the one revelation of the Qur'ān, where he appears in numerous passages as an exemplar of genuine submission to God. Al-Baqara (2) 124-36 can be seen as an answer to the question – parallel to that faced by Paul – of the rightful membership of the community of Abraham.

Because of the presence and significance of Abraham in their three scriptures, Judaism, Christianity and Islam are sometimes grouped together under the common name of 'the Abrahamic religions'. While this may be a useful shorthand to indicate three traditions which share many themes and questions in common, it is not without its own problems. While the figure of Abraham does indeed appear in all three faiths, the texts and reflections below show that there are important differences in the way that his significance is interpreted. In Jewish tradition, he is primarily seen as the father of the nation of Israel, chosen to be God's instrument of blessing for the world; it is Noah, rather than Abraham, who is the prime exemplar of a universal covenant of God with humanity.[2] Both Christian and Islamic scriptures, by contrast, seek to provide a direct access for contemporary believers to the divine promise made to Abraham, through entry into his family or community. Nevertheless, the respective criteria which they offer for this universalizing are by no means identical.

Biblical text: Romans 4

[1]What then are we to say was gained by Abraham, our ancestor according to the flesh? [2]For if Abraham was justified by works, he has something to boast about, but not before God. [3]For what does the scripture say? 'Abraham believed God, and it was reckoned to him as righteousness.' [4]Now to one who works, wages are not reckoned as a gift but as something due. [5]But to one who without work trusts him who justifies the ungodly, such faith is reckoned as righteousness. [6]So also David speaks of the blessedness of those to whom God reckons righteousness apart from works:

> [7]Blessed are those whose iniquities are forgiven,
>   and whose sins are covered;
>
> [8]blessed is the one against whom the Lord will not
>   reckon sin.

[9]Is this blessedness, then, pronounced only on the circumcised, or also on the uncircumcised? We say, 'Faith was reckoned to Abraham as righteousness.' [10]How then was it reckoned to him? Was it before or after he had been circumcised? It was not after, but before he was circumcised. [11]He received the sign of circumcision as a seal of the righteousness that he had by faith while he was still uncircumcised. The purpose was to make him the ancestor of all who believe without being circumcised and

64

who thus have righteousness reckoned to them, [12]and likewise the ancestor of the circumcised who are not only circumcised but who also follow the example of the faith that our ancestor Abraham had before he was circumcised.

[13]For the promise that he would inherit the world did not come to Abraham or to his descendants through the law but through the righteousness of faith. [14]If it is the adherents of the law who are to be the heirs, faith is null and the promise is void. [15]For the law brings wrath; but where there is no law, neither is there violation.

[16]For this reason it depends on faith, in order that the promise may rest on grace and be guaranteed to all his descendants, not only to the adherents of the law but also to those who share the faith of Abraham (for he is the father of all of us, [17]as it is written, 'I have made you the father of many nations') – in the presence of the God in whom he believed, who gives life to the dead and calls into existence the things that do not exist. [18]Hoping against hope, he believed that he would become 'the father of many nations,' according to what was said, 'So numerous shall your descendants be.' [19]He did not weaken in faith when he considered his body, which was already as good as dead (for he was about a hundred years old), or when he considered the barrenness of Sarah's womb. [20]No distrust made him waver concerning the promise of God, but he grew strong in his faith as he gave glory to God, [21]being fully convinced that God was able to do what he had promised. [22]Therefore his faith 'was reckoned to him as righteousness.' [23]Now the words, 'it was reckoned to him,' were written not for his sake alone, [24]but for ours also. It will be reckoned to us who believe in him who raised Jesus our Lord from the dead, [25]who was handed over to death for our trespasses and was raised for our justification.

Notes on Romans 4

1. An alternative translation would read: 'What then shall we say? Have we discovered Abraham to be our forefather according to the flesh?'

3. Paul refers here and throughout this passage to the account of God's blessing of Abraham in Genesis 15, especially 15.6 ('He believed the Lord; and the Lord reckoned it to him as righteousness').

10. The account of Abraham's circumcision in Genesis (ch. 17) is narrated subsequent to the account of his blessing (ch. 15).

13. The promise that Abraham would 'inherit the world' is not drawn from Genesis 15, where the inheritance of Abraham's descendants is rather precisely delimited according to the ideal boundaries of David's empire (Genesis 15.18b-21). Rather, Paul may be liberally interpreting the later promise of Genesis 17.5 that Abraham would be made 'the ancestor of a multitude of nations' – certainly he goes on directly to quote this verse in 17 and 18.

Commentary on Romans 4

This chapter has sometimes been read by Christian theologians[3] as one of the most important sets of proof-texts for the doctrine of 'justification by faith alone'. Rather than approaching it as a didactic exposition, though, we can see Paul's argument as a reflective elaboration (*midrash*) on Genesis 15, telling the story of Abraham's blessing by God, promising to him and Sarah a great progeny. The question which Paul is addressing is that of the identity of this progeny, who are inheritors of the promise made to Abraham. In other words, Abraham is here first and foremost a protagonist in the narrative of God's people.

For Paul this narrative certainly finds its decisive turning-point in the death and resurrection of Jesus Christ. Remarkably, however, Jesus is not mentioned until the penultimate verse of the chapter – and, even then, in a passive sense, as the one whose raising from the dead by God demonstrates the identity of the God in whom true faith is to be placed. Rather than focusing on the figure of Jesus, Paul's argument here emphasizes that faith in this God is the essential feature of Abraham's response to God which can be shared by contemporary believers, enabling them in turn to become characters in the continuing story of God's people.

The identification of faith as the criterion for association with Abraham's blessing means that the promises made to the patriarch are universalized in two dimensions. On one hand, the 'family of Abraham' is no longer to be conceived as his descendants 'after the flesh': it constitutes a fellowship truly 'of many nations', in that all who share in his faith in the God who raises the dead are to be counted as members, whatever their ethnic or religious background. At the same time, the geographical significance of the promised land of Israel (exactly specified as such in Genesis 15.18b-21) is replaced for Paul by the gift of 'the world' – that is, the whole earth – to this community of faith.

Qur'ānic text: al-Baqara (2) 124-36

> [122]Children of Israel, remember how I blessed you and favoured you over other people, [123]and beware of a Day when no person

can stand in for another. No compensation will be accepted from him, nor intercession benefit him, nor will anyone be helped. [124]When Abraham's Lord tested him with certain commandments, which he fulfilled, He said, 'I will make you a leader of men.' Abraham asked, 'And will You make leaders from my descendants too?' God answered, 'My pledge does not hold for those who do evil.'

[125]We made the House a resort and a sanctuary for people, saying, 'Take the spot where Abraham stood as your place of prayer.' We commanded Abraham and Ishmael: 'Purify My House for those who walk round it, those who stay there and those who bow and prostrate themselves in worship.' [126]Abraham said, 'My Lord, make this land secure and provide with produce those among its people who believe in God and the Last Day.' God said, 'As for those who disbelieve, I will grant them enjoyment for a short while and then subject them to the torment of the Fire – an evil destination.'

[127]As Abraham and Ishmael built up the foundations of the House (they prayed), 'Our Lord, accept (this) from us. You are the All Hearing, the All Knowing. [128]Our Lord, make us devote ourselves to You; make our descendants into a community that devotes itself to You. Show us how to worship, and accept our repentance, for You alone are the One who accepts repentance again and again, the Most Merciful. [129]Our Lord, make a messenger of their own rise up from among them, to recite Your revelations to them, teach them the Scripture and wisdom, and purify them: You are the Mighty, the Wise.'

[130]Who but a fool would forsake the religion of Abraham? We have chosen him in this world and he will rank among the righteous in the Hereafter. [131]His Lord said to him, 'Devote yourself to Me.' Abraham replied, 'I devote myself to the Lord of the Universe,' [132]and commanded his sons to do the same, as did Jacob: 'My sons, God has chosen religion for you, so make sure you devote yourselves to Him, to your dying moment.'

[133]Were you (Jews) there to see when death came upon Jacob? When he said to his sons, 'What will you worship after I am gone?' they replied, 'We shall worship your God and the God of your fathers, Abraham and Ishmael and Isaac, one single God: we devote ourselves to Him.' [134]That community passed away. What they earned belongs to them, and what you earn belongs to you: you will not be answerable for their deeds.

[135]They say, 'Become Jews or Christians, and you will be rightly guided.' Say (Prophet), 'No, (ours is) the religion of Abraham, the upright, who did not worship any god besides God.' [136]So (believers) say, 'We believe in God and in what was sent down to us and what was sent down to Abraham, Ishmael, Isaac, Jacob and the Tribes, and what was given to Moses, Jesus and all the prophets by their Lord. We make no distinction between any of them, and we devote ourselves to Him.

Notes on al-Baqara (2) 124-36

124. Abraham is described as a 'leader of men' – the word 'imām', used also for the person who leads the Muslim community's prayers, has connotations of leadership, exemplarity and paradigmatic status, as well as conveying a sense of divine appointment.

125. 'The House' refers to the sanctuary at Mecca, the ka'ba; the 'spot where Abraham stood [maqām ibrāhīm]' has traditionally been identified with a particular small building in the sanctuary. Abraham is to 'purify' a sanctuary which is already in existence – according to Āl 'Imrān (3) 96, it is the 'first house appointed for humanity'.

128. The phrase 'make us devote ourselves to you' could also be translated 'make us Muslims'; the reference is to the act of submission to the divine will which is the essence of Islam – the same meaning is present also in verses 131 and 132.

130. Millāt ibrāhīm, here and in 135 translated as 'the religion of Abraham', indicates the actually existing company of monotheistic believers submissive in the same way as him – it could equally well be rendered as 'the community of Abraham'.

Commentary on al-Baqara (2) 124-36

Abraham is presented in these verses as one chosen to be an exemplar for humanity, through his single-minded submission (islām) to God. A similar rectitude is in fact to be found among his family, but the passage makes clear that physical descent from the patriarch is not sufficient to ensure God's blessing: rather, this is reserved to those who make the same submission as Abraham. Although verse 125 describes how Abraham foreshadows the liturgical practices of the Meccan pilgrimage, it seems that the spiritual attitude being spoken of here should not be narrowly identified with the religious community of 'Islam' taken in the restricted sense of those who follow the religious ordinances revealed in the seventh century to the Prophet Muhammad. Rather, it appears to indicate the wider sense of an obedient response to the essentially unchanging divine message given to all the prophets, including Abraham. Those who are entitled to share in the benefits for which

Abraham prays are those who manifest in their lives this pattern of obedience, which finds its perfection in the practice of the Islamic religion. In this way, the Qur'ān provides a way of universalizing access to the 'community of Abraham', while at the same time balancing this with the specificity of the revelation of God through Muhammad to which Abraham points forward.

Thus, while this passage presents monotheism as the primordial truth repeatedly declared to the world through constant prophetic admonition, with Abraham featuring as a paradigmatic exponent of authentic religion, its teaching is set within an overarching framework of narrative. Thus, looking back, Abraham's action at Mecca is to 'purify' a sanctuary already given to humanity from the beginning; looking forward, his prayer for a 'messenger' from among the Arabs finds for Muslims its fulfilment in the prophetic mission of Muhammad.

The Meccan sanctuary further demonstrates the universal aspect of Islam, in that it is explicitly intended by God to be a place of spiritual resort for all humanity. While the specific geography of the city is an invariable divine given, access to it is not restricted on grounds of ethnicity or nationality, but rather is made open to all who are submissive to the divine revelation.

Reflection 1: Blessings for all humanity

Both the biblical and the Qur'ānic passages present Abraham as a figure whose blessing by God is available to a wider group than that of his physical descendants – indeed, according to both the latter have in some ways failed to live up to the promise extended to their forefather. Positively, Romans 4.16f. argues that the true 'family of Abraham' comprises those who share his faith in the God who raises the dead, while al-Baqara (2) 135 implies that the 'community of Abraham' is defined by those who share his monotheistic submission to the one God without any associates. Although the transition is made in different ways, both texts can therefore be seen as offering a reinterpretation of the patriarchal Abraham of Genesis in the direction of a more universal model for all humanity, who in turn can have access into the divine favour which Abraham enjoys through identifying themselves with him in his covenanted relationship with the God who was revealed to him.

Moreover, both texts draw out geographical as well as sociological con-sequences. Not only is membership of the people of God in principle accessible to all, but there is also a corresponding broadening of the idea of a location where the reality of the divine will is focused: the 'land of promise' of Genesis 15 has in Romans 4.13 been expanded to cover the whole earth, while Mecca according to al-Baqara (2) 125 is to be a sanctuary for all humanity. In actual fact, in the working out in religious history of these scriptural starting points, both traditions have demonstrated a certain ambiguity about the sense of sacred place. In Islam, the centrality of Mecca has coexisted with an emphasis on the availability of any location to serve as a venue for prayer and a pointer towards the divine, while in practice access to the holy cities has been restricted to members of the historically constituted Muslim community. In Christianity, popular spirituality has insisted on celebrating Israel-Palestine as 'holy land', not primarily because of its status within the divine promise but through its being the locus of God's saving deeds. By extension, local sites related to the lives of holy men and women have also played important parts in both Christian and Muslim devotional histories, while always theologically being referred back for their fullest meaning to a wider frame of reference.

In these senses, therefore, the two texts have a parallel spiritual dynamic: both display the energy of a God who opens up our local and limited loyalties to a more universal sense of belonging. However, this very parallelism should prevent any facile harmonization of their two accounts of Abraham's significance. Precisely because both religions propose to believers ways of associating themselves with his blessing, they can in some sense be seen as being in competition with one another, so that Abraham himself becomes a contested figure. This tension arises from the marked difference in the two criteria proposed in either case for identification with Abraham's family or community. In the case of Christians, this is a sharing in his faith in the God who raised Jesus from the dead, a revelation of divine power so gratuitous that it can only be recognized through an unmerited and unexpected divine gift of faith to the believer. For Muslims, the identifying factor is obedient submission after Abraham's pattern to the divine will and fulfilment like him of the divine commands, yet this behaviour in some sense expresses the natural inclination and purpose of men and women as created. This distinction should not indeed be pressed too far – the mainstream of Christian theology has never denied the important role played by the free human will in coming to faith, while Islam has always acknowledged the continuing reality and power of the ignorance (*jāhiliyya*) which obscures the clear light of monotheistic reason – but the difference of emphasis cannot be ignored.

Reflection 2: Gospel and guidance

The two texts considered here can be read within either an exemplary or a narrative frame of interpretation. According to the former, Abraham would be an essentially timeless paradigm of certain religious qualities to be replicated in believers – whether the faith which leads to justification, or the perfect obedience of submission.

According to the latter, Abraham would be a key character in the developing plot of the story of the divine engagement with humanity – whether as the patriarch who receives the promise which is to be fulfilled in the resurrection of Jesus Christ, or as the purifier of the sanctuary whose prayer points forward to the coming of the Prophet Muhammad. These two ways of interpreting the passages are by no means mutually exclusive; in fact, it could be argued that elements of both need to be brought together to do justice to the rich and many-layered resonances of the scriptural texts.

Nevertheless, it does seem that, in contemporary scholarship at least, narrative approaches seem generally more congenial to Christians, exemplary approaches to Muslims. These differences may arise in part from the different situations, needs and attitudes of Christian and Muslim communities today; but they may also reflect more deeply divergent emphases in ways of understanding the central proclamation of either faith. Thus, a narrative approach coheres naturally with the announcement of the Gospel as 'good news', a message about the new opportunities offered in human history by the God who 'calls into existence the things that do not exist' (Romans 4.17). On the other hand, an exemplary approach fits well the exposition of Islam as the guidance along the path of obedient submission and upright behaviour repeatedly made known by God through a succession of prophets of whom true Muslims can say that 'we make no distinction between any of them, and we devote ourselves to Him' (al-Baqara (2) 136).

This distinction between 'gospel' and 'guidance' cannot indeed be pushed too far, and should not be over-systematized, but a recognition of the tensions involved in these two approaches may help both Christians and Muslims to a fuller appreciation of their differences as well as the things they hold in common. The figure of Abraham, the righteous recipient of God's promise and friendship, is a potent symbol both of our common faith in a God of universal concern and of the mutually contested ways in which we understand access to that God's blessing.

The ethics of gender discourse in Islam

Mona Siddiqui

In this essay, I give a brief overview of the intellectual and literary elements that have shaped the discourse on gender and women in Islam, and of some of the contributions that have been made. Where are we now as Muslims, and why are we still having some of these debates? Is there a next stage, or have we gone as far as we can – in relation to scripture, at least? Perhaps the essential core of the debate has now moved beyond academic comment to individual social and political organizations which are steering this debate in a variety of ways.

For both Islam and Christianity, many of the challenges of the present are essentially the challenges of what is loosely known as modernity. Modernity should not be viewed as antithetical to traditional religion, but both modernity and modernism are in some ways a stark challenge to traditional attitudes to religion and to traditional religious systems, since one of the central questions of modern times is, how we arrive at a meaningful interface between the Divine and the secular. These two positions are not to be seen in opposition to each other, as very often they traverse each other's boundaries, but they do often bring different approaches to our most complex human concerns. Over the last fifty years or so, the world as a whole has witnessed a certain fragmentation of organized religion, but despite the formal removal of religious ritual from many areas of public and private life, and despite the many political and ideological waves that have come and gone, the major religions of the world have managed to come through these challenges, not because they could provide all the answers to emerging problems, but because their theologies essentially embody two very human needs: a sense of hope and conviction. If anything, Islam has succeeded in drawing more and more people to itself, and emerged numerically a much stronger world religion. Now in the postmodern era, it is viewed as a truth amongst many truths – this is the theme that lies at the centre of postmodernity. The religion has taken on different guises, different reflections and different tones, all struggling to reflect, devise and live the true Islam, and all relatively susceptible to modernizing influences.

But this Islam has a rich and varied past, an intellectual tradition that constantly had as its reference point the search for defining God's will. In fact, the history of the Islamic intellectual tradition developed on the premise that all the varying oral and written traditions were somehow a reflection of the need to analyse God, or man's relationship to God.

The many different styles of pious reflection – *kalām, fiqh, tafsīr, tabaqat, sīra* and so on – are examples of how scholars tried to make sense of a revelatory process that for them saw a formal seal to revelation with the death of the Prophet, yet emerged as a living socio-intellectual phenomenon only through interpretation and comment of the living community of subsequent generations. These works and disciplines, along with others, form an Islamic canon of some sort, to which the faithful return for meaning, and which are subject to the whole process of selection and revision through different generations and cultural communities. They are both history in the making and history unfolding, since they are the written legacies of the faithful trying to understand revelation, and at the same time this literary intervention aims to open up the past, to provide a continuous link with the sacred.

Thus, it is this history that has formed the backdrop of so many Muslim societies. This textual backdrop is ultimately the only authority in Sunni Islam, and within it the traditional understanding of law or the *sharī'a* is pivotal in providing legitimacy to much of the normative belief and practice within Islamic cultures. But in recent years, many Islamic scholars have urged that this law, this vast fabric of pious intellectualism, is not divinely ordained but a human construct. Even though this human endeavour was essentially trying to say what the Qur'ān was saying, it remained a human endeavour, and the Qur'ān remains not a book of law – a word which has so many layers of meaning in the Islamic tradition – but, in its own words, a 'book of guidance'. If this book of guidance is to retain an eternal and relevant message to the believers – and that is a major reason why God intervenes in history – it must be approached with honesty and with courage, to shake off some of the conventional patterns of behaviour that, because they based themselves on selected readings, may be seen as repressive or unjust, and in order to search for an insight that will be the inspirational basis for a more ethical Islamic practice today.

Nowhere has this been deemed more urgent and necessary than on the issue of gender relations in Islam. The whole gender debate in Islam has focused specifically on select verses of the Qur'ān. Like all the monotheistic scriptures, the Qur'ān has been reproached for gender bias in favour of men, and then the subsequent traditions within all the law schools have in varying degrees been accused of fossilizing this discrimination, and thereby condemning women to a lesser status than men. Until recently, the juxtaposition of the very words 'female' and 'Islam', or 'women' and 'Qur'ān', were enough to provoke either

73

extreme contempt or sympathy, since this issue was seen as a separate context within the Islamic faith – by many, as Islam's worst feature, by others, as its most misunderstood. Depending on the perspective, the rhetoric was either apologetic or critical; yet once the debate had begun to make an impact – largely through the political nationalisms that emerged in the period after the Second World War, bringing with them modernist ideas, that is, Western political and social values – it soon became obvious that the changes that were being advocated would have a ripple effect on the whole model of Muslim societies.

In fact, from the nineteenth century onwards, the benchmarks for conservative or liberal Islam resulted in large part from the discussion of women's status. Some of this came, naturally, as a result of the colonial impact and the observance of what was happening with various women's movements in Europe, but the thrust of the overall discourse of women's roles in society came from within Islamic societies, and formed the foundation of subsequent academic debate in the Western and Islamic worlds. Three or four core issues began this discourse, and still form the main themes running through contemporary debates: polygamy; the concept of the word *qiwama*;[4] the verses dealing with *ḥijāb* or veiling. All other issues, such as marriage, divorce, abortion, and family planning, seem to remain subservient or at a tangent to these core dilemmas. The starting point for any discussion remains, without a doubt, the Qur'ān and the *ḥadīth*.

The *Salafiyya* movement founded by Jamal al-Din al-Afghani (1838–97), and continued by his disciple Muhammad Abduh (1849–1905), was one of the first movements which had as its aim a return to the Qur'ān, yet Abduh's modern *tafsīr* of the Qur'ān questioned those areas of *muʿāmalāt* that were now corrupt, or should no longer be applied for the moral progress of the Muslim community. On polygamy, he has been considered the first theologian to reinterpret the Qur'ānic verse that deals with four wives:

> A nation that practises polygamy cannot be educated. Religion was for the benefit of its people; if one of its provisions begins to harm rather than benefit the community . . . the application of that provision has to be changed according to the changed needs of the group.[5]

Abduh, Afghani, and even Syed Qutb (who died in 1965) came to the same issues from differing perspectives, and despite daring to question this whole framework they walked a tightrope between conservatism and the new Islamism that wanted to Islamicize modernity, and not to modernize Islam. Mohammed Shaltut, the rector of al-Azhar, emphasized that what was needed was a new kind of *tafsīr*, that looked at the Qur'ān not line by line but as a whole, to pave the way for a new social morality. This call for different epistemologies led many scholars, such as the Pakistani Fazlur Rahman, to argue that the *sharī'a* too was a historical construct, and thus could be reconstructed for contemporary needs. The fact that it would still be rooted within the Qur'ān would thus show how the Qur'ān could continue to be of eternal inspiration to Muslims.

One of the central concerns was women's dress. An enormous amount has already been said on this single issue, yet it is still as important today as it was in the early stages of the debate. Women's clothing was about women's honour, and this in turn was about the social morality of the Muslim community. So in the nineteenth century, Arabs who had either visited the West or been educated in the West, such as Qasim Amin and Rifa'at Thatawi, targeted particular issues, and in their own way championed what they saw as new avenues opening for women. Amin focused on the veil, and female seclusion in general, as indicative of the social backwardness of Islamic societies. Unless women were educated in a formal sense, Arab society would not truly prosper. Huda Asharawi (died in 1947), the founder of the Egyptian Feminist Union, was to emphasize this unease even more when she took the veil off in public on her return from the International Union of Women in Rome. The whole debate was complex and highly charged, and remains so even today – as can be seen from some of the writings of Fatima Mernissi, who claims that not only is veiling and segregation not grounded in the Qur'ān, but that since the abolition of slavery only women and minorities are left as a test for the state to modernize itself and bring its laws into conformity with the principle of equality it claims as a fundamental value. Women may not be the political leaders of the Islamic world, but they are always a political tool. Furthermore, it should be understood that there is enough diversity of opinion and conflict on these matters within different women's groups and organizations: this is not a male-female conflict, but rather a conflict of interpretation and tradition.

Even if we concede that these very stances presuppose a view of women as an undifferentiated mass, and of Islamic culture as a monolith, we can say that what lay at the forefront of these emerging concerns was a reassessment of a worldview on a truly global scale. This reassessment demanded that muted voices speak and be heard not through the dualistic and antagonistic framework that lay at the core of some forms of feminism, but through a direct escape from binding social mores contained within the ultimate truths and divine commands known throughout the Muslim and non-Muslim world as the *sharīʿa*, God's law. Thus women's voices did start to speak out, questioning from a female perspective, from a female view of history and scripture, why the totality of humanity had only partially been recognized, only partially been free, and in the end been totally silent except for containing exemplary and glorified figures who lived either in an idealized past – such as the Prophet's youngest wife ʿĀʾisha, his daughter Fatima, and the mothers of the believers in general – or in the Qurʾānic narrative – such as Mariam or Bilqis. On the one hand, these figures provided select evidence for the argument that women had not been absent from the development of Islam as a culture and civilization, that they had in fact made a significant contribution to the genesis and spread of Islam; but on the other hand, they also highlighted how subsequent centuries of Islamic thought had deliberately disengaged ordinary believing women as much as possible from both public and other central arenas of society. It was argued that the androcentric interpretation of scripture which had permeated the political and the personal areas of Islamic societies both fed into and fed off the patriarchal ideologies upon which so much of Islam was institutionally established. It was further maintained that in the area of personal law – the laws of marriage, divorce, child custody and so on – women had been unjustly discriminated against because male interpretation had so forcefully, subtly and successfully convinced Islamic familial and social structures that this was God's will, God's prescribed moral and social order, where women had a rightful place, any movement from which might well be a compromise of their virtue and honour.

When this whole debate took on its own life force with Islamists and particularly women, working mainly through academic institutions or human rights organizations, it soon became apparent that what lay at the very foundation of the new debate was the need of Islamic societies for new interpretations of scripture. Scripture contained an ethic and a morality that had remained largely hidden because it suited men, who had always been the legislators, the reformers, and the public face of piety. These writers were calling for a reading of the Qurʾān, and to some extent the words of the Prophet, which would emphasize this hidden morality: a scripture that implied justice had been used to promote discrimination; a scripture that recognized difference had been used to create hierarchy; most importantly, a scripture that encouraged compassion amongst believers had been used for covert degradation. Women had been written about, especially in the legal works, but they had never really been the contributors, the voices that shaped discourse.

There was only one reason why this had happened: this was a universal situation, not specific to Muslim women but applicable to virtually all the major religions – specifically, to Western Christianity, where women had much earlier realized in different ways that they too had been either absent from or silenced within the theological constructs of early Christianity. In the many forms of feminism that arose from the Western Christian world, one area was that of feminist biblical interpretation, which had as an underlying premise the insistence that the emancipation of women required liberation through texts.

Biblical texts and the canons of early Christianity, alongside other historical sources, needed to be revisited for the sake of a more just and honest society. Hitherto, the manner in which these sources had been interpreted had resulted in the marginalization of women in virtually all forms of life – social, political and spiritual. What was imperative to a new vision was the revisiting of scripture, shifting the parameters, according dignity and credibility where both had been denied. Women interpreters knew that the task of initiating this new dialogue lay primarily with them. In rereading scriptures with new *midrashim*, and emphasizing the contribution that women had made to early Christianity and to the formation of Christianity as a world religion, a dignity could be salvaged. The maleness of the Christian faith in all its aspects gave way to a different future, where gender bias would be replaced by an essential equality asserted as the basis of a new spirituality and social theology of God's ideal moral order.

This short comment on one aspect of feminist debate within the Christian world is not intended to simplify or to obscure the issue of gender concerns in Islam, but merely to emphasize that there lie common issues relating to women in society that go beyond cultural and religious affiliation. Different faiths have their own ways of dealing with this most dramatic challenge of contemporary times; what must be recognized is that this is a challenge that cannot be met without making scripture the basis for a continuing dialogue with God which must then return to society in new and more compassionate ways.

If feminist aspirations and grievances are united worldwide by common causes relating to marriage, family, employment and sexuality, there are also some real differences in approach that emanate from a variety of settings – for example, whether the resurgent voices speak within rural or urban settings, within educated elites or illiterate masses. One other crucial factor is the internal dynamics of different faith systems – what have been the core concerns within each religion, how they manifest themselves, how significant has been the impact upon them of modernizing ideas. Unlike Christianity, where the central theological concern was the doctrine of God, in Islam this doctrine (or its parallel) was a limited debate, eventually affirming the Ash'arī position of the complete omnipotence and otherness of God – God as completely transcendent, deserving of human worship but beyond human knowledge: the doctrine of God began and ended with an affirmation of God's absolute and complete unity.

What was really of interest to Muslims, though, was how to obey this God. One of the basic models according to which Muslims have regarded themselves in relation to their Creator has been that of the master and slave, *rabb-'abd*. The way in which the Qur'ān has been understood through the years is that it is only through obedience that we can do the right thing and obtain God's mercy and favour. The Qur'ān is replete with verses relaying this message time after time: obey God and act righteously – obedience then becomes the highest form of virtue. This obedience, however, was not confined to *'ibādāt*, 'worship' in a ritual sense, but extended to the whole range of *mu'āmalāt*, all human activities. The desire to understand what was expected of us in everyday life resulted in the mass accumulation of *fiqh* writing – essentially, understanding God's law, which then became synonymous with the concept of *sharī'a*. This was to prove the major theological activity of Muslim scholars in the classical period, revisited and sometimes modified through the centuries in the works of muftis yet remaining within the traditional understanding, using traditional tools and carefully observed. With no clerical hierarchy in Sunni Islam, no central focus of authority, the jurists were setting the parameters of discourse, both defining and refining the detail, exercising judicial artistry as well as faithful devotion. Abdullahi an-Nai'm states quite accurately:

> To describe the founders of *sharī'a* as scholars and jurists does not mean that they had formal qualifications for interpreting the Qur'ān other than their own learning and integrity as judged and accepted by the community. They were neither certified by any person, body or institution as qualified interpreters to the exclusion of others, nor did they claim such a status for themselves. They were simply acknowledged by Muslim communities through a very gradual, spontaneous and informal process of acceptance and following or rejection of their views by contemporary and subsequent communities.[6]

It is precisely because this law was a form of interpretation that so much of it is sifted and weighed within communities and by governments.

Thus we find that, in the recent changes resulting from modernity, Muslim governments worked with colonial legacies and borrowed from their former masters in many areas of political, economic and legal life. This had the effect of imposing change upon society, as it very often supplanted the conceptual framework of the *sharī'a*. Yet in one area this change was limited, in some countries non-existent – and that was in the area of women in society. In those areas that affect women as a whole, family laws continued to remain largely within the domain of a more conservative system of *sharī'a* law. Women were thus living surrounded by change, and often contributing to this change, but walking a tightrope between what they saw as new and rightful opportunities yet opportunities which were offered with reservation and which often came with criticism.

In the nineteenth century, women were being defined, rather than being allowed the opportunity to define themselves. They were being placed in categories; depending on the nature of their work or the slant of their approach, the labels of 'secular' or 'religious' were being placed upon them. Ultimately, the fact that women had become more visible in public life did not really mean that their more diverse activities had become more acceptable, even if it could be argued that the Qur'ān had never delimited the scope of women's activities, or even prescribed the domestic setting as the ideal. This again has parallels with Western cultures, where – despite contemporary images of equality in rights and opportunities – there are still more obstacles and boundaries for women than for men. In the twentieth century, however, women in general are speaking from recognized positions from where their voices can be heard. Headway has been made not only by women (and male) scholars who have argued in the socio-academic terrain – such as Afkhami, Mernissi and Bouthains Shaaban – or looked at the theological grounding of gender issues – such as Stowassers's excellent work on 'Women in the Qur'ān' – but also by women at grass roots level, who may not be grounding their concerns in academic rhetoric but are nevertheless applying measures according to what they see as issues of human rights and ethics, rather than being inhibited by an immobility arising from religious parameters. Curiously, a big problem remains that of support – not just from those in positions of power, but from other Muslim men and women, who remain convinced that any change from accepted practice is a deviation from divine truth, and thus to be resisted and condemned.

This is where we are now: beyond the initial debates, struggling to find how we can reread scripture with an emphasis on the ethical norms which must serve as a basis for our continuing dialogue with God. If it comes to selecting readings, how do we make this selection, and do we give our new reading a social and moral momentum? The diverse lifestyles that Muslims are now leading is witness to the fact that choices are being made and decisions taken, within and outside of public discourse. Yet issues that continue to challenge our morality, including sexual morality, have at times been moved to different spaces. The challenge of modernity for Muslims is not Westernization – the East–West bipolarity is a smokescreen – but rather the challenge of interpretation and meaning: keeping God's word alive in a world of competing interests, making sure that we do not hide behind our scriptures, but face them with courage and, above all, humility.

A Circle perspective

Esther Mombo

Phyllis Trible, in the foreword to her celebrated work, *God and the Rhetoric of Sexuality*, provides an interesting piece of information. Trible informs us that according to the Old Testament scholar, Brevard S. Childs, the publication of *Honest to God* by Bishop J. A. T. Robinson marked the end of biblical theology as a major force in American theology.[7] This is indeed a pregnant observation. We can go as far as to say that if Bishop Robinson had not dealt the death-blow to biblical theology – and its orientation to a cold, objective and impersonal historical-critical methodology of interpreting the Bible – in the early sixties, we might not have been in a position now to meet as Christians and Muslims to discuss interpreting the scriptures as we face legacies of the past and challenges of the present.

My purpose in this paper is twofold. First, I would like to underscore the complexity of thought and rational tradition that underlies the seemingly simplistic term 'hermeneutics', and to trace the historical mutation of biblical interpretation through the centuries. Secondly, I shall attempt a brief bibliographical analysis of certain publications of the ecumenical and inter faith body of African women theologians called 'The Circle', identifying their core concerns in relation to the issue of interpreting the scriptures.

Hermeneutics and interpretation: the subtle distinction

A subject like 'hermeneutics' is not easy to define. On the contrary, it is one of the most difficult subjects. Such difficulty emerges from at least three factors.

The first factor is that 'hermeneutics' and 'interpretation', although widely treated as the same, are really not synonyms. Interpretation is indeed the *task* of hermeneutics, but hermeneutics is not interpretation. Hermeneutics has been defined as the 'theory of interpretation'. Hence we may say that, while hermeneutics is not interpretation, it is actually interpretation of interpretation![8] This means that hermeneutics seeks to interpret what goes on into the process of interpretation. This is a serious restriction. It means that we really cannot use such terms as 'liberative hermeneutic', 'feminist hermeneutic', 'Black hermeneutic', and so on, unless we are prepared to go into philosophy and tackle the question of what – from the point of view of philosophical theory – *goes into* the process of interpreting the Bible or theology from a liberative, or a feminist/womanist, or a Black perspective.

This brings us to the second factor. Hermeneutics as an academic discipline belongs to at least three areas – philosophy, theology, and the Bible. Of these, philosophy is the basic root of hermeneutics. The philosophical foundations of hermeneutics rest on the pillars of epistemology (the theory of knowledge), linguistics (the theory of language), semantics (the theory of meaning), and semiotics (the theory of interpreting symbolism). Each of these pillars in itself constitutes a vast and complex body of knowledge. This is why it is almost impossible for us to talk of any 'hermeneutic' unless we are able to tackle the underlying philosophical issues of what, why, and how we are trying to interpret something.

The third factor is that, even if we succeed in isolating the philosophical, theological and biblical strata from within the complex whole of hermeneutics, we shall still need to recognize the inescapable reality that each of these strata, in itself, is a complex whole. It is this reality to which F. D. E. Schleiermacher drew our attention, for the first time.[9]

Biblical interpretation through the centuries

The history of biblical interpretation, from the early church period, via European history up to the modern times, indicates a mutation. This mutation starts with the 'text-centred' approach of the early Church, and moving via the 'author-centred' approach in the European history, finally culminates into the modern 'reader-centred' approach. In other words, this mutation can be seen beginning with the textual hermeneutic (Alexandrian School), and then moving via the historical-critical method (European schools), reaches the sociometric and contextual approaches prevalent in modern times, especially the reader-centred approaches pertaining to the currently popular variables of gender, race, and economic class. Various Western philosophers have guided this mutation through its various stages.[10]

Going back to the early Church times, the chief interest of the church fathers was with the biblical text itself, and not so much with the authorship. Authorship was a matter of general and commonly agreed assumption – the Pentateuch by Moses, the Psalms by David, and the Wisdom writings by Solomon, and so on. Also the early church fathers seem to have been interested basically in recovering the real meaning of the biblical text rather than reconstructing its original form (something later done by text critics). The basic method of interpreting the biblical text was *allegorical* (Origen, Augustine and Jerome). This meant that biblical language was not to be interpreted literally but symbolically, with the object of recovering its deeper meaning. On the analogy of the human personality comprising body, soul and spirit, Origen argued that biblical language also has a similar three-tier structure – that is, words, meaning and deeper meaning. Although challenged by the Antiochian School, the allegorical interpretation continued to enjoy a prime place among early church fathers.

With the development of modern rationalistic philosophy in the sixteenth century (the Cartesian School) and the Protestant Reformation, two things happened. First, there was a resurgent interest in the Bible; second, there was now a rational approach to interpreting the biblical text. Under rationalist Jewish scholars like Baruch Spinoza and Ibn Ezra, the earlier assumptions – for example, that Moses wrote the Pentateuch – were subjected to rational scrutiny. Within the next three hundred years (sixteenth to nineteenth centuries), biblical interpretation had taken a definite direction in Europe, especially in Germany. Kant's critique of pure reason, although giving a new direction to philosophical pursuits, did little to deter biblical critics from their intellectual interest in biblical interpretation. The launching of the philosophy of history by Hegel ushered biblical interpretation into a dimension that was to remain determinative for the next century. Now biblical scholars were fully obsessed with history: reconstruction of the history of Israel, historical reconstruction of the biblical text, historical reconstruction of the authorship of various biblical books. The result was the development of the so-called 'historical-critical method' and its unchallenged rule in the field of biblical interpretation until the middle of the twentieth century. So, we can say that whereas the approach of early church fathers to biblical interpretation was basically 'text-centred', that of the latter Western scholars was 'author-centred'.

The second half of the twentieth century has witnessed a new focus in the approach to biblical interpretation. Now, the once celebrated historical-critical method has been brought into sharp critical focus and even vigorously assaulted. Theology has been restored to a new, normative orientation, and the Bible is seen not merely as an ancient text offering intellectual recreation in terms of reconstructing an ancient history, but as Scripture to which contemporary men and women can turn to solve their real life problems. It is this new turn in the history of theology that Trible has referred to as Bishop Robinson's 'monumental iconoclasm'. However, in any talk of 'Robinson's death-blow to biblical theology', and to the impersonal objectivism of the historical-critical method, which characterized biblical studies for nearly two hundred years, three sobering points must be borne in mind.

First, what we may rather melodramatically refer to as a 'death-blow', is not so much a death-blow to biblical theology as such, but to a heartless, impersonal, and almost arrogant objectivism that biblical theology perpetrated across the affluent West for nearly two centuries. Biblical scholars in the poorer nations of what was once commonly referred to as the 'Third World' were duped into believing that unless they applied the historical-critical method, they could not know the Bible. The historical-critical method is still used in most colleges in teaching exegesis partly because of 'colonization of the mind', to use Ngugi wa Thiongo's contention.

Secondly, the current clamouring against the historical-critical method of biblical theology does not mean that Robinson's work has taken us back to the days of dogmatic theology, so that we can now afford to forget J. P. Gabler and his monumental contribution.[11] Far from it! Gabler brought the Bible back into focus, and there it still remains. If anything, the Bible today is under greater and sharper focus than it was before. Only the focus has now shifted: from the objective to the subjective, from the descriptive to the normative, from problem-analysis to problem-solving, from 'pure' to 'applied'. An instance is the work of Itumeleng J. Mosala, who is sensitive to the methodological issues underlying the hermeneutical problem. Mosala has taken pains to give a critique of both the social-scientific and historical-critical methods before approaching the subject of biblical hermeneutics from a materialistic-subjective point of view.[12] This is in line with other

African scholars who were trained in historical-critical methods of biblical studies, but parted ways in their writings. Their hermeneutical approaches have been termed as *inculturation, indigenization, Africanization, contextualization* and *adaptation.* Rather than being involved in the recovery of the authors' original meaning or the context of the biblical authors, the African scholars insisted on finding similarities between the Bible and African culture. The Bible in this case was being read from the perspective of the scholar's context. This was, to return again to the word of Ngugi noted above, 'decolonization'.

Thirdly, despite the worldwide emergence of various liberation theologies in our times, and despite the emergence of various 'liberative hermeneutics' (from the gender, race, and socio-economic perspectives), the historical-critical method has not been completely discarded. It is taught in the theological seminaries of the South, and continues to influence the biblical interpretation of many scholars.[13] So here we are, with all our problems and issues, trying to interpret the Bible in a normative way. We want to solve our gender problems and our culture problems – all in the light of a biblical interpretation that can suit us within our own particular context.

It is in this sense that the currently popular approach to biblical interpretation may be termed as 'reader-centred'. Now the Bible has to be understood and interpreted in terms of the readers' specific situations – *their* problems, *their* needs, *their* anxieties and so on. This new approach has been readily embraced by liberation theologians in their quest for reading and understanding the Bible in a manner that can liberate women and men from oppression on the basis of gender, race and class. It is in this context that we look at biblical interpretation from the perspective of women from the Circle of Concerned African Women Theologians (in brief, 'The Circle').

The Circle: African women theologians and biblical interpretations

The Circle was inaugurated at Trinity College of Theology, Legon, Accra, Ghana in 1989. It is an ecumenical and inter faith body of African women theologians tracing their background to such organizations as the Ecumenical Association of Third World Theologians (EATWOT), the Ecumenical Association of African Theologians (EAAT), and the Conference of African Theological Institutions (CATI). However, the Circle is different from the other ecumenical bodies, whose membership is predominantly Christian. Members of the Circle include women who belong to Christianity, Islam and indigenous African religions. Members of the Circle are engaged as individuals and groups in writing articles and books on various topics of theology.[14] The Circle has regularly held meetings in various parts of Africa since its inception in 1989, and has published its conference proceedings following each meeting.[15] Reading and interpretation of the Bible is a major study for the Circle publications – reading and interpreting the Bible done in the context of the African women, which includes violence and multi-faith contexts.

Ways of reading and interpreting the Bible

The Bible, which is regarded as the authoritative and normative witness to divine revelation, provides Christianity with its dominant narratives, images and symbols. These are taken up in preaching, teaching, prayer and doctrine and thus play an extraordinarily powerful part in shaping the religious consciousness of believers. But for most women, this is acutely problematic. For the Bible was written and created by men in patriarchal culture and largely reflects a patriarchal world order. Women reading the Bible find issues such as the invisibility and the inferiority of women in the scriptures. There is also the sexism of the processes of translation and interpretation.

It is in this context that Western feminists have wondered whether the Bible could ever liberate women from a patriarchal, male chauvinistic, system of oppression.[16] Western feminists would even challenge the traditional understanding of the Bible as the revealed Word of God: 'How can the Bible be the Word of God if it legitimizes and commands female suppression? Is it not shown to be merely the fallible words of men? If we proclaim that oppressive patriarchal texts are the Word of God, then we proclaim God as the God of oppression and dehumanisation.'[17]

Phyllis Trible in her *Texts of Terror* highlights the biblical stories of the abuse, rape, murder and dismemberment of women.[18] This, further to the questioning of the Bible as the word of God by writers from the West, attempts to come to terms with the damaging and negative biblical traditions about women. It is in this context that E. S. Fiorenza proposes a fourfold method for interpreting Scripture: a hermeneutics of suspicion, a hermeneutics of proclamation, a hermeneutics of remembrance and a hermeneutics of creative actualization.[19]

The book *Searching the Scriptures* (in two volumes), a collection of essays from around the world, contains significant discussions by women hermeneutists from the South. The first volume features theologians such as Rita Nakashima Brock, Ada Maria Isasi-Diaz, Kwok Pui-Lan and Teresa Okure. The volume contains a record of the development of feminist interpretation, critiquing patriarchal methods and suggesting appropriate ways forward. The second volume features the argument that patriarchy led to the suppression and exclusion of women-empowering texts from the canon. The volume highlights some of these texts, and also attempts to recover a tradition of 'Sophia submerged in the canon'. Unlike some of the Western feminists, the Circle theologians favour a restored focus on the Bible and an interpretation of the Bible in the context of the African women. This context includes the social, cultural and multi-faith context.

Writing about feminist interpretations in Africa, Teresa Okure notes that:

> African women's distinctive approach to biblical interpretation is doing theology from women's perspective. This approach has distinctive characteristics of inclusiveness, it takes note of both men and women in interpreting scripture, it also includes both scholars and non-scholars, the rich and the poor, it is also inclusive of the scientific, the creation and popular methods.[20]

Okure's study *The Johannine Approach to Mission: A Contextual Study of John 4:1-42* has contributed to inculturation, biblical hermeneutics, African feminist, and international forums of feminism. Her articles on volumes that dealt with social location and with recent feminist trends represent the voice of Africa.

In their writing the Circle members seem to have parted ways with some of the Western neo-Marcionite radicals who have rejected the authority of the Bible. Even before the inauguration of the Circle, the eminent African feminist, Professor Mercy Amba Oduyoye, had argued:

> As a woman who feels the weight of sexism I cannot but go again and again to the stories of the exodus, exile and to other biblical motifs in which 'the least' are recognised and affirmed, are saved or held up as beloved of God or at least are empowered to gnaw at the fundaments of the structures of injustice until these fundaments cave in on themselves. These narratives have been for me the bearer of good news. Therefore in spite of entrenched patriarchal and ethnocentric prepositions of the Bible, it is a book I cannot dispense with and indeed may not since I remain in the Christian community and that community means more to me than my personal hurts.[21]

During the inauguration of the Circle, Musimbi Kanyoro noted that:

> The Bible is a message of liberation for African women, much as it is also used to deny their freedom. During the Bible sessions it became clear to us that for women to find justice and peace

through the texts of the Bible, they have to try and recover the women participants as well as their possible participation in the life of the text. Secondly women will need to read the scriptures side by side with the study of cultures and learn to recognise the boundaries between the two. Such recognition will help women to interpret biblical passages within the proper hermeneutical understanding of ourselves and our contexts as Christian women. Women will need sincerely to claim biblical liberation without being apologetic to the culture set-up in which the message of the biblical passage has found its audience.[22]

The major thrust of Oduyoye and Kanyoro seems to be that the Bible as such is *not* an instrument of oppression of women, so much as a lopsided interpretation of the Bible, vested with ulterior motives. Therefore, women do not really need liberation from the Bible as such but from an oppressive *interpretation* of the Bible.

Although women from the Circle are aware of what the women from the West are saying and writing about the Bible, they examine the issue of biblical authority from their own reality. Teresa Okure argues for a distinction between timely truth in the Bible and its cultural underpinnings. Rereading the Bible as a patriarchal book demands that sustained efforts are made to discern between the divine and the human elements in it. For while the former embodies timeless truth for our salvation, the latter inculcates practices that are socio-culturally conditioned, hence inapplicable universally.[23] In her study of John 20.11-18, she rejects the interpretation that the phrase 'do not touch me' (17a) implies that pollution would result from Jesus being touched by a woman; on the contrary, the phrase implies no rebuke but rather is part of Mary's commissioning.[24]

Hence one should not be surprised to find a twenty-page Appendix to the Circle publication *Transforming Power* containing a comprehensive list of biblical texts pertaining to women's contexts. Nyambura Njoroge's expounds 1 Samuel 1 – 2 from a Kenyan woman's perspective, and Margaret A. Umeagudosu's develops the biblical theme of 'The earth belongs to God' from a Nigerian woman's perspective. More recent studies include Mmadipoane, on *Bosadi*/womanhood, post-apartheid feminist hermeneutics,[25] and Musa W. Dube on postcolonial feminist hermeneutics.[26] Other methods include storytelling, divination, gender-inclusive and postcolonial biblical translations, cultural hermeneutics (Musimbi Kanyoro) and HIV/AIDS biblical hermeneutics.

Storytelling is a method used mostly by women to re-enact history, to instil moral discipline and to pass on information. Storytelling as a method of reading the Bible re-enforces the 'reader-centred' aspect of interpreting the Bible. In her article 'Fifty years of bleeding', Musa Dube uses two stories to interpret Mark 5.24-43, which is a third story. The two stories include an African oral tale of a young girl who is buried by her friends but sings from her grave, telling her story. The second is the story of Africa in the past fifty years, covering the pre-colonial, globalization and the colonial periods, the struggle for independence and independence, and the neo-colonial, globalization and AIDS periods.[27]

For members of the Circle, their biblical interpretation is determined by the context in which they live and work. The context includes that of survival in harsh conditions of oppression, exploitation and male dominance. Therefore the reader-centred approach to scripture is more appropriate than the 'historical-critical method', which downplays the social context of the reader, thus making the Bible alien. Since the Bible has played a significant part in the life of the church in Africa, it has also played a very important role in the socialization of women and in determining their place in the church and society.

Biblical interpretation and an objective critique of African culture

As noted earlier, African scholars' methodology for interpreting the Bible is through inculturation. This method was meant to do away with the way in which colonial Christianity suppressed African culture as uncouth and uncivilized. Inculturation hermeneutics was indeed a process of reading for decolonization that sought liberation by asserting the diversity and similarities of African cultures and the Christian tradition.

It was partly meant to challenge colonial Christianity, which legitimized the suppression of African and other world cultures. Inculturation's purpose was to ensure that the gospel is spread to Africans in their own languages and symbols, to the extent that some of the inculturation readers tended to be more interested in turning African cultures into vehicles for spreading the gospel rather than in recognizing them as cultures in their own right. While inculturation was and is still an important method of biblical interpretation, for members of the Circle, inculturation fails to critique aspects of African culture which are both discriminating and oppressive to women. It is in this context that reading the scriptures is done in the context of an objective critique of African culture.

Writing about the interpretation of the Bible, Musimbi Kanyoro has rightly observed that:

Popular Bible readers do not really care what the scholars think. They read the Bible with their own cultures and they apply a mirror image reading. Sometimes the Bible helps read their cultures while other times their culture gives meaning to the texts of the Bible . . . All questions regarding the welfare and status of women in Africa are explained within the framework of culture. Women cannot inherit land or own property because it is not culturally right. Women may not participate in the leadership because it is culturally the domain of men.[28]

In interpreting the Bible, Circle writers take serious note of the different cultures that are in the continent and how they impact women's lives. It is in this light that I talk about biblical interpretation and an objective critique of African culture. I call it an *objective* critique simply because the Circle writers have neither advocated a complete rejection of African culture, nor a blind apology for it (as, perhaps, was the case with 'negritude' enthusiasts). The Circle writers seem to prefer the same balanced and selective criterion for critiquing the African culture that they adopted for biblical interpretation.

Therefore, on the one hand the Circle writers have sought to expose the oppressive strands within their native culture. Musimbi Kanyoro, for example, in a paper published in a Circle (Kenya Chapter) volume, has observed that 'culture has silenced many women in Africa and made us unable to experience the liberating promises of God'. In an objective vein, Kanyoro concedes that there are 'favourable aspects of our culture which enhance the well-being of women'. Unfortunately, though, '[Such aspects] have been suppressed. [And] those aspects which diminish women continue to be practised by various degrees by our societies, often making women objects of cultural preservation.'[29] Kanyoro then recounts two moving case studies featuring, pathetically, women's plight caused and legitimized by African culture. It is within this context that Kanyoro has argued that cultural hermeneutics is significant in analysing both the African context and in reading the Bible.[30]

Hazel O. Ayanga's study of tracing violence against women in African oral literature is another illustration of how the Circle writers are concerned about the cultural condoning of women's oppression in Africa.[31] Mary Getui attempted a study of naming ceremonies in her native Abagusii community with special reference to women, and concluded that 'as far as naming and naming process is concerned women are getting a raw deal'.[32] Similarly, another Kenyan Circle writer, Grace Wamue, has highlighted the plight of widows caused by cultural taboos with special reference to her own Agikuyu community.[33]

On the other hand, the Circle writers have also sought to recover the positive aspects of African culture. Getui, for example, has attempted to show that not all African culture has been oppressive, in her paper entitled 'The Grandmother in the African traditional household: lessons for today'.[34] Similarly, Hannah Kinoti has argued that certain traditional African practices were helpful to the society. She has done this illustrating her case from the Gikuyu practice of *Nguiko,* which aimed at regulating the sexual behaviour of boys and girls, and thus protecting girls against sexual assault.[35] Another Circle writer, Elizabeth Amoah, has argued that in her native Akan community there was a religious relationship between humanity and nature.[36]

In line with this positive appraisal of African culture, the writers on hermeneutics from the Circle have analysed both the Bible and the African cultures in which it is used. In the first volume the Circle published, *The Will to Arise*, women analyse the different situations of women in Africa and how culture is used to determine their position.[37] Some of the cultural aspects that are written about in this volume include practices such as female circumcision, polygyny and some forms of levirate marriage. These issues are not new but they are problems that affect women, and the Bible seems not to be clear or is silent about them. But since women's position is defined by culture, these issues need to be looked at in that light.

Biblical interpretation and a concern towards violence against women

Biblical interpretation for members of the Circle is in the context of issues that affect women. While there are social, economic and political issues, they are summarized here under violence against women. In her book, *Texts of Terror*, Phyllis Trible analyses the biblical texts that appear to justify violence especially against women. How can these texts, which are damaging and negative towards women, be God's word? It is the awareness of such texts that has given rise to the Circle writers' concern with violence against women.

Violence is a culture-specific phenomenon. It might connote different meanings in different cultures. Anything from hurting someone's feelings, to inflicting grave physical injury could be termed as 'violence'. In an African context, the term 'violence' usually refers to inflicting grave physical injury. Cases of school children dying as a result of 'caning' by teachers, and wives sustaining serious injuries as a result of 'being disciplined' (read 'being beaten mercilessly') by their husbands, are usually reported in African dailies, and read with the apathy of routine life. Thus, unfortunately, violence against women is a sad reality of African social life. Naturally, therefore, if reading and interpreting the Bible, or doing theology, has to make any tangible sense to African women, then it cannot be done in isolation from the sad reality of violence against women.

In line with the above legitimate concern, it would only be expected that the Kenya Chapter of the Circle devoted an entire volume to the theme of *Violence Against Women* (1996). I have already mentioned the articles by Ayanga, Kanyoro, Njoroge, Getui, Kinoti and Wamue appearing in this volume dealing with the theme of violence against women from different perspectives. The remaining three articles deal with the theme as follows: 'Rape as a tool of violence against women' (Margaret Gechaga), 'A theological reflection on economic violence against women' (Constance R. A. Shisanya) and 'The Church in Africa and violence against women' (Ruth Muthei James).

The following year (1997) witnessed the publication of two Circle volumes entitled, respectively, *Where God Reigns* (ed. Elizabeth Amoah) and *Transforming Power* (ed. Mercy Amba Oduyoye). The former has a whole section (the entire third part) devoted to violence against women. The five articles in this part are entitled: 'Widowhood beliefs and practices of the Avatime' (Rebecca Ganusah), 'Women and widowhood rituals in Nigeria: the traditional Igbo society' (Angelina U. Umeh), 'Violence against women: the issue of domestic violence' (Veronica I. Okeke), and two similarly titled articles 'Violence against women' (one by Dinah B. Abbey-Mensah, and the other by Eunice Ekundayo).

The latter Circle volume *Transforming Power* (1997) has devoted the following two articles to the issue of violence against women: 'Infant mortality and related religio-cultural violence against women' (Daisy Mwachuku) and 'The status of women in the traditional African rites of passage: the religio-cultural roots of violence against women' (Ncumisa Manona).

The above rather rapid bibliographical survey would suffice to show how seriously concerned the Circle theologians are about the issue of violence against women. Writing on violence is one way of bringing the issues to light, which otherwise have remained unexamined. Since the Bible is significant in African Christianity, analysing issues of violence in the light of scripture demystifies them, allowing them to be analysed and looked at critically with a view to taking action. The issues of violence cease to be abstract but are treated as real.

Biblical interpretation and taking cognisance of the multi-faith context

Our world is a multi-faith context. The Circle is different from other ecumenical bodies whose membership is predominantly Christian. Members of the Circle include women who belong to Christianity, Islam and indigenous African religions. The Circle reflects some African families where you have members of one family belonging to different religious traditions. The Circle theologians take cognizance of their multi-faith context.

Women in Asia and Africa exist in a context of religious plurality and the way they are defined within their religions has a lot of similarities. They do not opt for such a context by their free choice. They just find themselves coexisting with people of other faiths. Such inter faith partners may be neighbours, workmates, socio-economic colleagues (for example, a grocer, a butcher, a milkman, an employer, or an employee belonging to another faith than your own), and even relatives by marriage. In some cases such an inter faith social context provides a rich opportunity, to its members, of mutually enriching one another's faith. In other cases such a context presents its own difficulties and challenges the members to learn either to convert others to their own faith, or to coexist peacefully with people of other faiths.

Naturally, any reflection on the Scriptures, or any attempt at doing theology in such a situation, will require as a prerequisite to take serious cognizance of the surrounding inter faith context. The Circle theologians are conscious, to some degree, of their inter faith context. Such a consciousness is indicated from the fact that in almost all their publications there is at least one article by a Muslim woman. Hence the volume *Where God Reigns* (1997) contained an article entitled 'Islamic understanding of creation: the place of woman' by Rabiatu Ammah. The same author contributed an abstract entitled 'Women in a multi-faith context: a Muslim perspective' in another Circle volume entitled *Transforming Power* (1997). Ammah's approach is descriptive and – understandably – mildly apologetic.

An earlier Circle volume, *Groaning in Faith* (1996), contained a contribution by another Muslim woman writer, Sa'diyya Shaikh. The contribution is entitled 'The veil: a feminist theological analysis'. Shaikh's approach is characterized by an open mind, critical analysis, and objective enquiry. She has considered the traditionalist, fundamentalist, and modern approaches to Qur'ānic hermeneutics, and appears sympathetic to the modern, reader-response oriented, Gadamer-type of approach to interpreting the Qur'ān in such a way that it can guide modern men and women in their current social contexts. Such a modernist hermeneutical approach would facilitate the 'fusing the horizon' (using Gadamer's terminology) of seventh-century Islamic Arabia with the horizon of twentieth-century men and women.

While the inter faith orientation of the Circle is highly commendable, the Circle might need to include more contributions from its inter faith context – contributions from those belonging to other faiths and ideologies as well (Hinduism and African traditional religions and atheism, for example).

Conclusion

In this paper I have attempted to achieve two things. First, I have sought to analyse biblical interpretation itself with a view to tracing its history from its earliest (text-centred) to its latest (reader-centred) phases. Second, I have sought to attempt a bibliographical analysis of certain Circle publications so as to show that the Bible is a significant book and is taken seriously. The reading and interpretation of the Bible is done in the context of taking seriously the situation of women such as violence and the multi-faith context. The Circle's contribution to biblical interpretation in relation to gender and culture is significant for African women. Its greatest significance lies in the fact that, instead of blindly aping Western feminism, it takes the specific African needs and context into serious account, and attempts to hammer out a system of reading the Bible and doing theology which can make primary sense to African women.

Scripture dialogue IV: Righteous women

al-Aḥzāb (33) 28-36; Proverbs 31.10-31

Both the Qur'ān and the Bible have been, and sometimes still are, interpreted in such a way as to lead to the subjugation and denigration of women. How is this undoubted fact to be analysed and tackled by contemporary Muslims and Christians? In both scriptures, it is possible to find passages which appear to have patriarchal tendencies, or to be embedded within patriarchal structures; it is also possible to find texts which are read by women as liberating and affirming. Nor is this only a question of the scriptures themselves: throughout the centuries, the vast majority of exegetes, whether scholarly theologians and jurists, or popular preachers and teachers, have been men, and the attitudes of all have been shaped by the cultural experiences and assumptions of their own societies.

To see how the scriptures can be read today in a way which builds up mutuality and respect between women and men, therefore, it is necessary to take into account not only the texts themselves but also the ways they have been and are put to use in community life, and the changed contexts in which we read them now. These complex and interlocking themes are explored with relation to two passages which have played a significant part in these debates: al-Aḥzāb (33) 28-36, a series of verses addressed first to the wives of the Prophet and then equally to Muslim women and men, and Proverbs 31, a portrait of an idealized Israelite woman.

Qur'ānic text: al-Aḥzāb (33) 28-36

[28]Prophet, say to your wives, 'If your desire is for the present life and its finery, then come, I will make provision for you and release you with kindness, [29]but if you desire God, His Messenger, and the Final Home, then remember that God has prepared great rewards for those of you who do good.' [30]Wives of the Prophet, if any of you does something clearly outrageous, she will be doubly punished – that is easy for God – [31]but if any of you is obedient to God and His Messenger and does good deeds, know that We will give her a double reward and have prepared a generous provision for her. [32]Wives of the Prophet, you are not like other women. If you truly fear God, do not speak too softly in case the sick-at-heart should lust after you, but speak in an appropriate manner; [33]stay at home and do not flaunt your attractions as they used to in the pagan past; keep up the prayer, give the prescribed alms and obey God and His Messenger. God wishes to keep uncleanness away from you, People of the (Prophet's) House, and make you completely pure. [34]Remember what is recited in your houses of God's revelations and wisdom, for God is all subtle, all aware.

[35]For men and women who are devoted to God – believing men and women, obedient men and women, truthful men and women, steadfast men and women, humble men and women, charitable men and women, fasting men and women, chaste men and women, men and women who remember God often – God has prepared forgiveness and a rich reward.

[36]When God and His Messenger have decided on a matter that concerns them, it is not fitting for any believing man or woman to claim freedom of choice in that matter: whoever disobeys God and His Messenger is far astray.

Notes on al-Aḥzāb (33) 28-36

30-32. These verses begin with a vocative which clearly indicates that they are addressed to the 'wives of the Prophet (Muhammad)'. It is a disputed question of interpretation whether verses 31 and 33 (without the vocative form) are also addressed specifically to the Prophet's wives.

32. 'The sick at heart': this seems to refer to a culpable inclination to take advantage of too apparently compliant an attitude from the Prophet's wives, though the precise import is far from clear. The warning may be directed against the group known as the 'hypocrites', who were hostile to Islam under a show of outward support.

33. 'Prayer' here is ṣalāt, the canonical prayers of the Muslim community. These are to be offered by the women addressed in this verse from within their houses.

35. The grammatical endings of the Arabic nouns in this verse explicitly – and unusually – set masculine and feminine forms side by side. Tradition records that the verse was revealed in this way in response to the protest of a woman believer that the Qur'ān in general addressed the masculine only.

Commentary on al-Aḥzāb (33) 28-36

The status of women in relation to men is a contested theme in contemporary Islam, and has also become a problematic issue in relations between Muslims and Christians. Much of the argument has centred on the content and interpretation of traditions attributed to the Prophet, but the exegesis of several Qur'ānic passages – including these verses – has also played a major part in the debate. It is clear that the way these texts are read will be shaped by the context of the reading, and the identity and concerns of the readers; these contextual factors in turn can help to uncover new emphases within the texts. In this passage, two different themes can be identified.

In four of the first seven verses, it is the wives of the Prophet who are the immediate object of address, and it seems reasonable to assume that this whole passage relates specifically to their situation. Given their husband's unique position of leadership of the Muslims, their own profile and behaviour carried particular political and community implications which would not be shared by other women – there was, for example, the ever-present danger of the internal enemies of Islam, the 'hypocrites', seeking to use them to further their own ends. Thus, it is possible to see the injunction to 'stay at home' as a way of safeguarding the security and well-being of the prophetic household in particular, and so of the wider community in general. On the other hand, the wives of the Prophet have also been seen as role-models for Muslim women, and their seclusion has been appealed to by some to justify the development of radically separated male and female societies in much of Islamic history. Different accounts of the relation between the domestic and the public, and of women's freedom to cross the boundary between the two, may thus appeal to different weightings of the 'exemplary' and the 'exceptional' in the behaviour of the Prophet's wives.

The following verse (35) is clearly distinguished from what goes before, by its unusual syntax as well as by its subject matter. It constitutes a powerful and radical statement of the identical spiritual responsibilities and rewards of men and women in relation to their common God.[38] This implies an approach to the theme of equality different to that presupposed by secular presuppositions: rather than setting up a measure to compare the relative status of men and women, the key themes to be considered are taken as givens within an orientation of the human person to God. This means that the virtues that God seeks, of humility, modesty, chastity and so on, are to be seen as human qualities rather than as being associated with gendered roles. This then leads naturally in the last verse to a reminder of the obligation of both women and men to show obedience to God and his Prophet – a theme running through this whole *sūra*.

Biblical text: Proverbs 31.10-31

> [10]A capable wife who can find?
> > She is far more precious than jewels.
> [11]The heart of her husband trusts in her,
> > and he will have no lack of gain.
> [12]She does him good, and not harm,
> > all the days of her life.
> [13]She seeks wool and flax,
> > and works with willing hands.
> [14]She is like the ships of the merchant,
> > she brings her food from far away.
> [15]She rises while it is still night
> > and provides food for her household
> > and tasks for her servant girls.
> [16]She considers a field and buys it;
> > with the fruit of her hands she plants a vineyard.

¹⁷She girds herself with strength,
> and makes her arm strong.

¹⁸She perceives that her merchandise is profitable.
> Her lamp does not go out at night.

¹⁹She puts her hand to the distaff,
> and her hands hold the spindle.

²⁰She opens her hand to the poor,
> and reaches out her hands to the needy.

²¹She is not afraid for her household when it snows,
> for all her household are clothed in crimson.

²²She makes herself coverings;
> her clothing is fine linen and purple.

²³Her husband is known in the city gates,
> taking his seat among the elders of the land.

²⁴She makes linen garments and sells them;
> she supplies the merchant with sashes.

²⁵Strength and dignity are her clothing,
> and she laughs at the time to come.

²⁶She opens her mouth with wisdom,
> and the teaching of kindness is on her tongue.

²⁷She looks well to the ways of her household,
> and does not eat the bread of idleness.

²⁸Her children rise up and call her happy;
> her husband too, and he praises her:

²⁹'Many women have done excellently,
> but you surpass them all.'

³⁰Charm is deceitful, and beauty is vain,
> but a woman who fears the LORD is to be praised.

³¹Give her a share in the fruit of her hands,
> and let her works praise her in the city gates.

Notes on Proverbs 31.10-31

The form of this passage is an acrostic poem: each verse begins with a different letter of the Hebrew alphabet in order.

10. 'Wife' could also be translated 'woman': the expression *ēsheth ḥayil* ('capable wife' or 'valorous woman') parallels phrases used of (male) military heroes (Exodus 18.21; 1 Samuel 31.12).

15. 'Her household' (*bēthah* – also in 21 and 27) is unusual in the Hebrew Bible, where a household is usually identified by reference to a patriarchal figure.

21-22. 'Crimson' and 'purple', because of the rarity of their dyes, are colours associated with royalty – here they demonstrate the dignity of the woman's household.

26. The woman's speech conveys 'teaching of kindness' – literally, the 'instruction' or 'law' (*tōrah*) of 'covenanted love' (*ḥesed*). These are also the realities conveyed in biblical understanding by divine speech, as is 'wisdom'.

Commentary on Proverbs 31.10-31

This passage, at the very end of the Book of Proverbs, is a comprehensive 'A to Z' of what were perceived by its author as the qualities of an 'ideal woman', her character drawn in opposition to the prostitute or adulteress of earlier parts of the book.[39] The woman of Proverbs 31 represents the proverbial figure of wisdom, to the extent that in verse 26 her speech is described by the qualities of the divine word itself. At the same time, she is depicted as an actual married housewife, and as such has been held up as a role model in traditional teaching: 'Proverbs 31 is the mirror against which every Christian woman must stand and face herself'.[40] Such an interpretation, which has generally been promoted by male preachers and teachers, is questioned or rejected by many today as promoting an unacceptable domestication and subservience.

The way in which this text is used to position the status of women will depend on the context in which it is read. In the decentralized context of post-monarchical Israelite society from which Proverbs probably derives, women would have been key figures in the productive power of successful households, which were the central units of a pre-industrial economy. There is certainly a distinction between the sphere of domestic activity, where she is pre-eminent (it is 'her household'), and the civic life of 'the gate' where her husband is to be found; at the same time, the dynamic of trade and exchange involves the woman in far-reaching and adventurous interactions beyond the home. With the advent of capitalism, though, the role of the home as the basic unit of a traditional economy is lost: a sharp line is drawn between 'private' and 'public', and the household becomes a place of consumption rather than production. In such changed contexts, a reading of these verses as dictating domesticity to be the place for women can effectively mean disempowering and devaluing their role in wider society.

Within the life of the home, this passage shows a certain mutuality within the relationships of husband and wife: she is as central to the proper functioning of the household as he is. This has been an important strand in the Christian understanding of marriage. In the last two verses, however, the focus switches decisively from the marital bond to the woman's direct relationship with God. Despite the fact that the portrait of the woman strikingly makes no reference to her participation in the community's worship, it is clear here that in a spiritual sense she is on the same level as a man, in so far as either of them lives in the 'fear of the Lord' (a state contrasted with any outward display). This principle of fundamental spiritual equality will be clearly restated in the New Testament: 'There is no longer male and female; for all of you are one in Christ Jesus.'[41]

Reflection 1: Social engendering and spiritual equality

Both these passages have a double emphasis. In the first place, certain women – a group of wives, an idealized figure – are described or addressed within a social locus where their gender role is clearly defined and circumscribed. In both cases, this involves a distinction between the limits of the domestic environment and the space of what might plausibly, if anachronistically, be called civic society. In the former, the woman occupies an honoured, even a pre-eminent, place; in the latter, it is men who are dominant. Even so, boundaries between these two spheres are not absolute: the fact that the wives of the Prophet are given such detailed guidance on conversation with men presumably indicates that the likelihood of such encounters is acknowledged, while the woman of Proverbs benefits from the network of commercial contacts which are integral to a household-based agrarian economy. It is in any case important not to read back uncritically into these verses distinctions between 'public' and 'private' which have evolved subsequently in societies shaped by either faith, particularly if such distinctions serve to stress the importance of the former and marginalize the latter. Both texts have indeed been used in this way to enforce a curtailment and devaluation of women's lives; but such readings cannot be justified in today's context when the effect of cultural and economic changes in shifting the domestic-civic boundary is recognized.

The other emphasis, appearing at the end of both passages, is a reorientation of aspirations and expectations towards God. On this level, it is clear, women are to be counted as equal to men in their ability to enter into a relationship with their Creator and to enjoy his favour; correspondingly, they share equal responsibilities. This teaching may appear to stand in a certain tension with the absence in both passages of any reference to the place of women in communal worship. The part which women can rightfully expect, and be expected, to play in the liturgy has in different ways been a contested issue within both Islam and Christianity, as well as in Judaism.[42] However, this does not in any sense detract from the reality of the religious life to which these women have access. Rather, it serves to strengthen the dimension of practicality in their piety, reinforced by the scriptural disparagements of ostentatious display. Throughout Muslim and Christian history, there have been strong currents of female spirituality which have sought to embrace some of these self-limitations, seeing in them a source of liberation and affirmation; other women, though, have rejected this approach as a diversionary irrelevance.

Reflection 2: Texts and contexts

Are these passages affirming and liberating for Muslim and Christian women, or do they serve to diminish and constrict them? It has proved easy through the centuries of faith to use texts such as these to justify the denigration of women, or even to condone violence against women – and interpretations of this kind are still to be found today. On the other hand, it is equally easy in the contemporary situation to dismiss, bypass or simply ignore challenging scriptures. What is important is to recognize that our relations to these holy texts lead to a process of questioning in both directions. Approaching them from our own context, we have to discern the elements within them which are specific to a given situation and those which are still of direct and universal application. What is the significance, for contemporary female believers, of injunctions addressed in the first place to a group of women in a special position of exemplary leadership in a nascent community of faith? How far in industrializing or post-industrial societies can we propose differentiated gender roles drawn from the ideal picture of a 'capable wife' at the pivot of a home-based economy? If the scriptures present messages designed to reshape and humanize the cultural patterns of the societies to which they were delivered, how do we respond to them in societies where cultural norms have shifted significantly? These questions are not rhetorical: they require a serious engagement with the texts, based on an honest awareness of the context out of which we are reading them.

Conversely, we in our own situation need to be open to being interrogated by the questions the texts pose to us. Can we recognize between men and women a genuine complementarity and mutuality which is not a hidden form of subjugation or disparagement of either by the other? Is it possible to deepen and revitalize our understanding of gender equality by orienting ourselves first of all towards the God who seeks the perfection of our shared humanity, male and female, Christian or Muslim? Can we read in the picture of an industrious and harmonious household presided over by a 'valorous woman' a critique of the contemporary global trading systems, where most homes in some countries have become centres of consumption rather than production, while in others the cohesion of the family unit is often destroyed by pressures which leave women to manage at home while men seek work elsewhere? Might we even see in the biblical woman's skilful distribution (*nomia*) of the goods of her household (*oikos*) a pointer to that divine *oikonomia* by which God would have us regulate the resources of our common human home were we to seek a more just economic system for our world?

Chapter 4

Scripture and the Other

As they seek guidance from their respective scriptures, Christians and Muslims today are both very conscious of the existence of the Other. This chapter begins with papers by Frances Young and Basit Koshul analysing some of the biblical and Qur'ānic material available in addressing this question. Detailed consideration is then given to two pairs of texts from both traditions – including 'difficult' as well more apparently 'affirmative' passages. Finally, an essay by Rowan Williams explores the theological implications for Christians of coming to terms with the Otherness of the Other. The archbishop's paper – originally delivered as a lecture at Birmingham University shortly after the seminar in Doha – highlights the importance of the exploration of difference as a legitimate area for inter faith dialogue.

Christian scripture and 'the Other'

Frances Young

What are the scriptural resources on which Christians may draw in considering attitudes to 'the Other', by which I understand in this context 'non-Christians'?

Attitudes have differed over the centuries, and the scriptures can be said to provide warrant for various different positions, including evangelization of those who do not believe and hostility to outsiders, as well as the transcending of boundaries. The books that make up the Bible came into their present form over hundreds of years, and themselves reflect differing historical circumstances. I shall consider first the Jewish books known to Christians as the Old Testament, then turn to the New Testament, and end with some reflections on interpretation in the modern period.

The 'Other' in the books included in the Christian canon as the Old Testament: Particularity and universalism in tension?

The Old Testament may be described as the library of Jewish classics. It encompasses stories about national origins, religious and social laws, more than one version of early Jewish history, together with poetry and literature. It is therefore specific to a particular nation and its self-consciousness. There were originally Twelve Tribes of Israel in a confederation, whose common history is depicted as including the Exodus from Egypt and the occupation of the Promised Land, but by the time the scriptures were put together ten tribes had been lost and only the Judeans remained. By the time the New Testament came into being, the Jews were scattered all over the then known world, but retained their common identity, written as it was into their sacred literature.

One key element in their story concerns their election by the God who gave no name other than 'I am what I am' (or 'I will be what I will be'), or 'the God of Abraham, Isaac and Jacob'. This God chose them and entered into a covenant with them: 'If you obey my voice and keep my covenant, you shall be my treasured possession out of all the peoples.'[1] Yet it is also deeply written into these scriptures that this God is the God of all the earth. The very words just quoted continue: 'Indeed the whole earth is mine, but you shall be for me a priestly kingdom and a holy nation.' The election of this people is set in a context which suggests that they have a role in the purposes of the one God of the whole world.

So the whole Bible begins with God's act of creation. Historians may seek to trace the process behind the texts whereby the particular god of these desert tribes was turned into the God who produced the whole universe, but the texts themselves present us from the beginning with one God who is the source of all being. According to these same texts, this is the God who chose Israel. It seems that a tension between universalism and particularity is written deep into what Christians call the Old Testament. However, it may be better to discern in this the way that the universal Creator God chooses to engage with the creation, namely through particularities.

The history of the chosen nation records warfare with 'others', with the expectation that God is on the side of his people. Yet the notion of God's universal oversight had an impact on the nationalist tendencies of the material. It is important to note the challenge offered by the prophets, who suggested that God's judgement on the people for not keeping the covenant would take the form of their conquest by the Assyrians, then the Babylonians. If God could discipline his people through other nations, God must hold the whole of humankind in his hands, whether they knew it or not. A generation or two after the capture of Jerusalem, the exiles in Babylon were told that God would now restore them to their land, and the agent would be Cyrus the Persian, who is even described as God's anointed one (Messiah).[2] The fact that their God is the God of the whole universe not only means that all of history somehow goes according to God's plan, but also that even those who do not know their God may in fact act on his behalf.

The universalizing tendencies of the scriptures are reinforced by the character of what is known as the 'wisdom literature'. This includes the books of Proverbs, Job and Ecclesiastes, as well as the books known as Ecclesiasticus and the Wisdom of Solomon whose Greek texts were part of the ancient collection canonized by the Church. Modern scholarship has demonstrated how close parallels are to be found between this literary tradition and, at first, the literature of the ancient Egyptians and Babylonians, then later, Hellenistic philosophy. The ancient Jews responded positively to the culture of the Ancient Near East and shared many ethical and cosmological ideas with others. All of the Jewish wisdom-literature affirms One God, Creator and Sovereign over all.

Positive responses to others are not confined to these universalizing elements in the canon. In the Law revealed through Moses to the people, the stranger residing among the Israelites has a special place. Although not part of the covenant people, the *gērīm* ('resident aliens') should be treated with respect, protected against injustice and violence, and have the same privilege of rest on the Sabbath.[3] 'A curse upon the one who withholds justice from the *gēr*, the orphan and the widow.'[4] Again like widows and orphans, the *gēr* has a right to the gleanings from grain, olive and grape harvests.[5] The *gērīm* are included in festivals, and were to be provided with food and clothing.[6] 'You shall not wrong a *gēr*, or be hard upon him; you were yourselves *gērīm* in Egypt.'[7] 'You shall not oppress the *gēr* for you know how it feels to be a *gēr*; you were *gērīm* yourselves in Egypt.'[8] The Israelite has the soul of the *gēr*. Key figures, such as Abraham and Elijah, are depicted as *gērīm*. Even God appears as a *gēr*.[9] Despite the nationalist focus of much of the material in the so-called Old Testament, there are features which encourage openness.

Furthermore, two books, Ruth and Jonah, specifically challenge exclusiveness. Ruth was the foreign daughter-in-law of an Israelite living in Moab. The story tells of her determination to stick with her mother-in-law, Naomi, when, after the death of her husband and two sons, Naomi decides to return to Israel. Ruth, the foreigner, supports her mother-in-law by gleaning the fields of a relative, who eventually takes her in marriage. There is no sign of embarrassment at the fact that the great king David was descended from this foreigner. Exclusiveness hardens in a later period, and Jonah was the response.

The book of Jonah

Jonah appears amongst the books of the Twelve Prophets, but it is a strange book beside them. Jonah is the unwilling prophet who runs away from God's call. God's call is to go to Nineveh, the capital city of the most powerful of Israel's enemies. Eventually Nineveh repents in response to his reluctant preaching, so God spares the city, and Jonah is completely put out. Already it would appear that this story is more like a satire than a history. The foreign city, unlike Israel, repents when a prophet is sent; and God is merciful to foreigners, where Israel faced destruction as result of God's judgement. That the story is a parable rather than history seems to be confirmed by the extraordinary incident where Jonah is swallowed and regurgitated by a whale. This book would seem to have been composed at a time when the exclusivist spirit was high – namely the post-exilic period in which the law promulgated by Ezra excluded marriage with foreigners.

A strong feature of the book is its affirmation of God's sovereignty over all of creation. God is aware of Nineveh's wickedness. Jonah heads off to Spain – the opposite end of the earth – to get away from the Lord, but he cannot escape. The Lord sends a storm. Jonah explains to the sailors, who want everyone to pray to their own god for help, that he worships 'the Lord, the God of heaven, who made land and sea'. The sailors are terrified and seek to appease this almighty God with sacrifice and service. Meanwhile Jonah has tried suicide, telling the sailors to throw him into the sea. God ensures that a large fish swallows him. Jonah's subsequent prayer suggests that the story is a 'literalizing' of common motifs found in the psalms and elsewhere – going down into the deep, with the waters rolling overhead, is a metaphor for dreadful hard times, despair of all sorts and even descent into Sheol, the realm of the dead. What Jonah realizes is the same truth as that taught by Psalm 139 – you cannot get away from God even if you go down to the world of the dead where most people supposed God's hand did not reach. God now ensures that the fish spews Jonah up on the beach. So Jonah obeys and goes to Nineveh, proclaiming that in forty days Nineveh will be destroyed. The people repent. The king orders fasting and prayer. God changes his mind. Jonah protests, even suggesting he had run away because he knew all along that God would not confirm his message, as he knew God to be loving and merciful, always patient, always kind, always ready to change his mind and not punish. The final incident reinforces the point about God's care for what he has created and his pity for the innocent. God is greater than Jonah wants to acknowledge.

This text would seem to underline the universalizing tendencies of the scriptures, and to challenge on theological grounds the way religious and nationalist communities tend to become exclusive.

Yet this was not the way it was read in the time of Jesus, who is depicted in the Gospels as saying that no sign will be given to his generation except the sign of Jonah. This teasing remark is interpreted in two different ways. Matthew's Gospel sees the three days and nights Jonah spent in the whale as a prophecy of the three days and nights Jesus would spend in the grave.[10] But he also suggests (followed by Luke)[11] that the people of Nineveh will condemn the contemporaries of Jesus on Judgement Day for their failure to repent. It is instructive to see how what I have perceived as the main message of the book of Jonah is not explicitly read from the text in the Gospels. Nevertheless, Christian reading of these books has always understood that Israel has indeed been a light to the Gentiles, as the truth about God passed to all nations through the Gospel of Jesus Christ, which fulfils that towards which these books were pointing.

The 'Other' in the New Testament

The New Testament is incomprehensible without the books which became the Old Testament. It presupposes the One God, Creator of all, whose name is beyond speech and whose ways are beyond knowledge. It presupposes the story of this God's engagement with humanity through the chosen people of God. It inherits a certain exclusiveness from the Jewish tradition from which it arose, yet it breaks across boundaries in various ways. It presupposes the fulfilment of prophecy, and a cosmic outlook fostered by apocalyptic motifs ultimately rooted in the prophetic traditions.

The fulfilment of prophecy

The fulfilment of God's promises runs all through the New Testament. The texts regard Jesus as the Messiah, the anointed one, who was expected to bring in God's kingdom. At a time when God's people were subjected to the Romans, dreams of a restoration of King David's throne lived alongside apocalyptic visions of God bringing an end to the cosmic struggle of the sons of light against the sons of darkness, coming to judge everyone, including those resurrected from the dead, and then recreating everything according to the divine will and purpose. Such hopes were projected onto Jesus despite the fact that his career did not exactly follow any current expectations.

It would appear that the early Christians adjusted their expectations, finding prophecies to fit, justifying Jesus' death on the cross and his future return as universal Judge and King. Other prophecies were found pointing to a new covenant, to the inclusion of Gentiles, and to the gift of the Spirit. The scriptures of the Jews were read as meaning that God had called the followers of Jesus to be the elect, purified and holy awaiting their redemption as the End-time approached. This had two consequences. One was the sense that there was a short time in which to gather the faithful from every nation – a kind of universalism, but also implying election from the present evil generation. The other was the sense that the Church was now the true people of God:

> You are the chosen race, the King's priests, the holy nation, God's own people, chosen to proclaim the wonderful acts of God, who called you out of darkness into his own marvellous light. At one time you were not God's people, but now you are God's people; at one time you did not know God's mercy, but now you have received his mercy.[12]

Such ideas were to have the legacy of supersessionism – the view that Christianity superseded Judaism. Thus tension between universalism and particularity seems to prevail as new boundaries replace old ones.

The 'Other' in the Gospels

Jesus is depicted in the Gospels as breaking across boundaries. A brief catalogue would include at least the following points:
1. The core commandments of Jesus are to love God and love our neighbours – indeed, even to love our enemies.[13]
2. Jesus clearly welcomed people who were marginalized in his society (such as lepers), including some who were regarded as sinners by the religious leaders of the time. He told parables about welcoming outsiders to the feast of the kingdom.[14]
3. Many stories indicate the openness of Jesus to people usually treated with suspicion because they were non-Jews, such as the parable of the Good Samaritan, or the healing the servant of the Roman centurion – a Gentile.
4. Jesus told people not to judge others, in case they were judged by God.[15]
5. Jesus told his disciples not to stop someone driving out demons in his name, even though he did not belong to the group of the disciples, because 'whoever is not against you is for you'.[16]

6. According to some versions of the story, Jesus 'cleansed the Temple' for the sake of Gentiles, protesting: 'It is written in the scriptures that God said, "My Temple will be called a house of prayer for the people of all nations." But you have turned it into a den of thieves.'

The mission to the Gentiles

The question whether Jesus was a Jewish prophet, sent only to the lost sheep of the house of Israel,[17] or brought a revelation to non-Jewish peoples (the Gentiles), was one of the most contested issues in early Christianity, and the New Testament bears the marks of this argument. The earliest Christian documents we have are the Epistles of St Paul. Two of these at least (arguably more) are preoccupied with the questions raised by the conversion of non-Jews. Paul argues strongly that Gentiles should not be required to take on the ethnic marks of a Jew in order to become members of the believing community. He was clearly up against strong opponents who argued that salvation through Christ presupposed being a loyal Jew, and therefore the Jewish identity-markers of circumcision and keeping Torah should be required, just as if they were proselytes to Judaism. (Christianity was not yet a distinct religion at this point.)

This debate again reflects tension between universalism and particularity. On the one hand, the mission to Gentiles implies that the Gospel is universal and not confined to Jews; on the other hand it encourages a strong differentiation between those who accept the gospel message and become believers and those, whether Jews or Gentiles, who do not. For the Pauline tradition, it is really important that a new humanity has been forged in Christ in which the old divisions between Jews and Gentiles have been healed and transformed. Yet new identity boundaries were rapidly undermining the implied universalism.

The cosmic Christ and the Gospel of John

In Pauline theology the cosmic dimensions of apocalyptic have shaped ways of conceiving the significance of Christ. The Gospel is about the one God, who created everything, acting to put right all that has gone wrong with the creation. In the early Pauline Epistles this means that to Christ has been delegated the role of the final Judge. By the later Epistles, the pre-existent Christ is seen as fulfilling the role of Wisdom as God's instrument of creation.

This development can be understood in the light of certain passages in the wisdom literature.[18] Not only does Wisdom appear as the one through whom God created, but God's Wisdom is treated as present in all of creation – indeed, in the souls of human beings.[19] The Wisdom of Solomon expresses the presence of Wisdom in creation in language that echoes that of the Stoic philosophers.[20] The difference is that for the Stoics the divine Logos was only immanent, whereas for this Jewish text God is transcendent and the immanent Wisdom is 'the breath of the power of God', 'a pure emanation of the glory of the Almighty', 'a reflection of eternal light', 'a spotless mirror of the working of God, and an image of his goodness'. Some of the Greek phrases in this text appear in the New Testament describing God's Son.[21]

There is a pattern of thinking here which the author of John's Gospel shares. In principle this attribution of cosmic significance to Christ bespeaks a universal outlook. Yet in the Gospel of John there is one definitive verse which, for many Christian believers, indicates that only through Christ is salvation possible. That text is: 'I am the way, the truth and the life; no-one comes to the Father but by me.'[22] Most Christians simply take the statement at face value as the authoritative word of Jesus, but my question is whether a different perspective results from setting this in its context. The statement appears in the so-called Farewell Discourses. Here Jesus is presented as speaking to the disciples alone, that is, to those who will recognize him as coming from the Father, and who later on, when the Spirit has led them into all truth, will understand the message of the gospel as a whole, namely, that he is the Logos or Word of God. Maybe this statement should be understood in the light of the Prologue to the Gospel.

The opening words of the Prologue assert that God was 'in the beginning'.[23] This picks up the opening words of Genesis, the very first words of the Bible. The biblical claim about the one true God, who is the Creator of all that is, thus provides the fundamental perspective. The Word is with God, and indeed is God – for it was through him that everything was made. Nothing has come into being without him. Life is in him, and life is light for humankind. Of course this 'Wisdom-like' Word is the way, the truth and the life, for all human creatures; and because of his relationship both with all created things and with God, how else could anyone have access to the Father?

According to the Prologue, the light shone in the darkness, and the darkness could not grasp it. The true light enlightens everybody. It was in the world, and the world came into being through it, but the world did not recognize it. Thus the Prologue sketches the drama of the story to follow. The Word of the Lord came to prophets, who were rejected. The Word of the Lord came in person, and was rejected. God's wisdom may be universal, but it is also contested. The glory of the Lord is revealed at the hour when Jesus was lifted up on the Cross. Those who recognize that glory are empowered to become God's children.

The Prologue might seem to evidence a tension between the particular manifestation of the Word in Jesus Christ and the universal presence of the Logos in all creation, but maybe this is again a case of the universal God choosing to work through particularities? Jesus is surely not the exclusive presence of the Logos, simply the full embodiment of the Word which was already given to the prophets, and was present in all wise persons of every culture. In the second century, Christian Apologists, such as Justin Martyr, would claim that Jesus was not just the fulfilment of all that the prophets pointed to, but also the fulfilment of philosophy – that the Logos was present in Socrates. In that sense Christ is the way, the truth and life to which all philosophy, all religion, strives.

Interpreting the resources in the scriptures

Implicit in the rapid survey I have offered are the problems of interpretation for Christian communities today as they seek models of relating to the 'Other' in their biblical resources. In conclusion let me articulate the most crucial issues.

Genuinely traditional ways of reading the scriptures have not survived modernity. The nineteenth-century conflict with science over the biblical account of creation reinforced the programme of uncovering the facts behind the texts and locating their meaning in the intention of the historical author. As a result Christian interpretation has been polarized, for at least a century and a half, between, on the one hand, those who are open to questions about the difference between us and the culture and understanding of the historical persons who wrote and compiled the biblical library, and, on the other hand, those who want to assert that every word of the Bible is literally true (that is, factually accurate), since it is directly and unproblematically the Word of God. For the former, Jonah is a parable; for the latter it is literal history, miracle and all. For both groups, the problematic statement in John's Gospel just discussed must be taken at face-value. For the 'fundamentalist' it means what it says; for the 'critic', it is to be explained as part of the outlook of the community from which this Gospel emerged, and the discussion about whether we act on its basis is another issue – as is the potential anti-semitism of this Gospel, which consistently blackens Jews in ways that many find unacceptable in the post-Holocaust era.

Both groups, I suggest, are reacting to modernity. Neither group represents traditional ways of reading the Bible. The interpretations of Jonah in the Gospels already indicate this: the earliest Christians saw 'types' and 'prophecies' everywhere in what they came to call the Old Testament. They also saw 'types' or exemplars of how to live in scripture and its narratives. Here was not a set of documents to be interpreted through archaeological research, but a body of literature from which, given the inspiration of the interpreter, the truth of God could be read. If the plain meaning created serious moral or theological problems, then the text was to be seen as pointing beyond its literal meaning to some spiritual truth. I believe we need to challenge modernity, particularly but not solely in its fundamentalist form, by reclaiming some of the methods, though not necessarily the results, of such traditional ways of reading scripture. This means allowing scripture to be read in the light of reason, universal moral values, and contemporary experience, under the guidance of the Holy Spirit and in prayerful commitment to find the way of Jesus for today.

For my part this includes uncovering the universalism of the scriptures, alongside affirmation of the gracious gifts we have received through Jesus Christ. It means repenting of Christian superiority, both its supersessionism and its exclusivism. The theological ground for this lies in a recognition of the transcendence of God, and the fact that God is immanent in the whole inhabited earth, with all its rich diversity. In the last analysis, that surely is what the Bible is about.

Affirming the self through accepting the Other

Basit Koshul

Reflections on the Qur'ān's treatment of the issue of the 'Other' can begin from a variety of standpoints. But whichever standpoint is chosen, it must take into account the context in which the discussion is taking place. The present discussion will begin by first identifying the present context (or parameters) of the discussion as being the modernist and postmodernist narratives. Both of these narratives provide their own models of how the Self should relate to the Other. The Qur'ānic model of the Self's relation with the Other will be presented in contradistinction to the modernist and postmodernist models. The discussion will detail how the Qur'ānic model embraces important aspects of both the modernist and postmodernist models, while at the same time transcending the limitations inherent in both. In conclusion

111

it will be argued that the life-giving breath of the Revealed Word provides resources that cannot be found in the modernist and postmodernist narratives. These resources make it possible to establish a genuine peace between the Self and Other by predicating an affirmation of the Self on an acceptance of the Other, something that neither the modernist nor the postmodernist narratives are able to achieve.

In the contemporary setting the two dominant paradigms that shape the Self/Other discourse are the modernist and postmodernist narratives. Because of the dichotomous dualisms and universalizing ethos that lie at the very heart of the modernist narrative, an unbridgeable divide is posited between the Self and the Other. An encounter of a Self with an 'Other' ultimately becomes a choice between either/or – either the one, or the other, with no room for relation or mediation. The logic underpinning the modernist narrative requires the Self to affirm itself through a marginalizing and negating of the Other. In this case the Self can only be at peace in the aftermath of a struggle in which the Other has been subjugated (or eliminated). The postmodernist narrative, as a critique and reaction to the dichotomous dualism of the modernist narrative, seeks to transcend all difference and efface the particularities that distinguish the Self from the Other. It is assumed that harmony and unity will replace conflict and tension with the erasure of difference and particularity. Postmodernism replaces the dichotomous dualism of the modernist narrative with a solipsistic monism that blurs all distinctions between the Self and the Other. The logic underpinning the postmodernist narrative requires an affirmation of the Other to such a degree that the Self is effaced and marginalized. In this case the Self can only be at peace in the aftermath of a struggle in which it has effaced itself (or completely eliminated itself) in the face of the Other.

In contradistinction to the logics of modernism and postmodernism, the logic of the Qur'ānic narrative predicates an affirmation of the Self on the conscious and willing acceptance of the Other. In the place of the dichotomous dualism of the modernist narrative and the solipsistic monism of the postmodern narrative, the Qur'ānic narrative is based on the logic of relational duality. The logic of the Qur'ān affirms the distinct identities of the Self and Other (*cum* modernism, *contra* postmodernism) and establishes reflexive relations between the Self and Other (*cum* postmodernism, contra modernism). This point can be illustrated by looking at the Self and Other, in the context of the Qur'ānic narrative, from three different perspectives: (1) the Qur'ān on Revealed Self and the Written Other; (2) the Qur'ān on

Scriptural Self and Scriptural Other; (3) the Qur'ān on Muslim Self and the non-Muslim (more specifically, the Christian) Other.

The very first āyāt revealed to the Prophet directly address the issue of the Revealed Self and the Written Other: 'Recite, in the name of your Lord who has created – created the human being out of a germ cell. Recite, for your Lord is the Most Bountiful One who taught the human being the use of the pen, taught the human being what he did not know.'[24] These words are the first revelatory encounter between the Prophet and the Archangel Gabriel – the introductory meeting, or the initiation of a relationship that will continue for the next twenty two years. It is worth pausing and looking at what the words say, and just as importantly what the words do not say. These words command the Prophet to 'recite' in the name of the Creator Lord who is the 'Most Bountiful One'. The description of the Creator Lord then depicts Him as the One who has taught the human being the 'the use of the pen' and by means of the pen taught the human being what the human being 'did not know'. What the words do not say is that the Creator Lord who is revealing these words to the Prophet is the same one who had previously revealed words to, among many others, Noah, Abraham, Moses, the Hebrew Prophets, Jesus (peace be upon them all). Subsequent revelations would repeatedly emphasize the fact that that which was being revealed to Muhammad (peace be upon him) is a continuation of the process that had produced the Torah, Psalms, Gospels, etc. In fact in some of the subsequent revelations it would be explicitly stated that one of the specific reasons for the Qur'ānic revelation was to confirm and affirm the previous revelations. In other words, it is a point of curiosity that in the first revelatory encounter, the Lord is not described as the same one who had initiated many such encounters previously – but rather as the Lord who had 'taught the human being the use of the pen'. The first Revealed Words heard by Muhammad (peace be upon him) in the cave of Ḥirā', affirm themselves by acknowledging and accepting an Other mode of Divine teaching and instruction – the art or science of writing. In short, the very first Revealed Words to Muhammad (peace be upon him) do not affirm themselves by establishing their linkage or relation to similar revelatory phenomena, but rather by acknowledging and accepting their linkage or relation to the Written Other.

The initial revelation to Muhammad (peace be upon him) recognizes the fact that the Creator Lord has two different modes of instructing human beings – by means of revelation and by means of the pen. At the same time it acknowledges the fact that whether knowledge comes to human beings through revelation or through the pen, the ultimate source is one and the same, the Creator Lord of the Universe. Commenting on the meaning and symbolism of 'the pen', Asad notes:

> The pen is used here as a symbol for the art of writing or, more specifically, for all knowledge recorded by means of writing . . . Man's unique ability to transmit, by means of written records, his thoughts, experiences and insights from generation to generation and from one cultural environment to another endows all human knowledge with a cumulative character; and since, thanks to this God-given ability, every human being partakes in one way or another, in mankind's continuous accumulation of knowledge, man is spoken of as being 'taught by God' things which the single individual does not – and indeed cannot – know by himself.[25]

This explication of the meaning of 'the pen' by Asad details the fact that not only does the Qur'ān as the Revealed Self acknowledge and accept the Written Other, the self-affirmation of Revelation takes place through the acknowledgement and acceptance of the Written Other.

While the very first words revealed to Muhammad (peace be upon him) bring the Revealed and Written Word into a mutually affirming relation with each other, the very first words in the Qur'ān bring different Revelations into relation with each other. If one considers the first *sūra*, *al-Fātiḥa*, to be a 'preface' or 'introduction' to the Qur'ān (its literal meaning is 'the opening'), the first passage in the Qur'ān is:

> *Alif Lām Mīm.* This Divine Writ – let there be no doubt about it – is [meant to be] a guidance for all the God-conscious who believe in [the existence of] that which is beyond the reach of human perception, and are constant in prayer, and spend on others out of what We provide for them as sustenance; and who believe in that which has been bestowed from on high upon thee, [O Prophet,] as well as in that which was bestowed before thy time.[26]

This passage begins with a pronounced self-affirmation of the Qur'ān as a book about which there is no doubt – no doubt that it is the Revealed Word, no doubt that it contains guidance for the God-fearing, no doubt of any kind about anything relating to it that the human mind may imagine. But, intricately woven into these profoundly self-affirmative assertions, is a self-critical distancing that makes it clear that the guidance contained in the Qur'ān is conditional. In order to benefit from the guidance contained therein, the individual has to be a person of faith (believe in that which is beyond the perception of the human being's physical faculties) and follow the legal dictate of religious teachings, praying, charity, etc. – but even this does not fulfil all of the conditions that an individual has to meet before he or she can benefit from the guidance contained in the Qur'ān. For further emphasis, it is added that in addition to the aforementioned conditions of faith and good works, the individual has to believe in what is revealed to Muhammad (peace be upon him) and believe in all of that which was revealed before this particular Prophet's time. Here the Qur'ān as Scriptural Self is affirming itself, by not merely acknowledging and accepting Other Scriptures (that which was revealed previously). It goes much further and makes the potentiality of its own guidance conditional upon the acknowledgement and acceptance of the Other Scriptures, by those who accept the Qur'ān to be Scripture. It is only those who believe in the Revelation 'bestowed from on high' on Muhammad (peace be upon him) 'as well as in that which was bestowed before' his time who will be able to get guidance from the Qur'ān.

There is a very different perspective of the Qur'ān's affirmation of itself through the acknowledgement and acceptance of Other Scriptures, than the one noted above. The Qur'ān does harshly critique the maculation and misinterpretation of previous Scriptures and calls upon the followers of the previous scriptural traditions to rectify these shortcomings in light of what is being revealed in the Qur'ān. But the Qur'ān's harshest judgement is reserved for those who accept neither its own authority nor the authority of the previous Scriptures. In quite clear terms the Qur'ān urges the followers of previous scriptural traditions to remain faithful to their own Scriptures, even in the maculated forms, because even these maculated Scriptures contain valuable guidance. The following passage illustrates this point very well *vis-à-vis* the Christian tradition:

> O followers of the Gospels! Do not overstep the bounds in your religious beliefs, and do not say of Allah anything but the truth. The Christ Jesus, Son of Mary, was but Allah's Apostle, His Word which He conveyed unto Mary, and a Spirit from Him. Believe then, in Allah and His apostles, and do not say 'Trinity'. Desist from this assertion for your own good.[27]

In even more clear terms the following passage paints a picture of those who 'truly observe the Torah and Gospels', when Allah speaks in the first person using the royal 'We' to address the followers of previous scriptural traditions:

If the followers of the Bible would but attain to [true] faith and God-consciousness, We should indeed efface their [previous] bad deeds, and indeed bring them into gardens of bliss; and if they would but truly observe the Torah and Gospels and all [the revelation] that has been bestowed upon them from on high by their Lord, they would indeed partake of all the blessings of heaven and earth.[28]

The following passage provides further evidence of the Qur'ānic Self accepting the Biblical Other. In this passage, when the believing Muslims are ordered by the Qur'ān to say to the adherents of the Torah and Gospels: 'Say: O people of the Book! You have no valid grounds for your beliefs unless you [truly] observe the Torah and Gospels, and al that has been bestowed from on high by your Lord.'[29] Whereas 2.1-4 sees the Qur'ān affirming its Scriptural Self by requiring Muslim believers to acknowledge, accept and affirm belief in (unspecified) Scriptural Others, the passages cited above evidence that the Qur'ān specifically and explicitly acknowledges and accepts the Biblical Other. As was the case with the Revealed Self and the Written Other, the Qur'ānic discourse with respect to the Qur'ānic Self and Biblical Other blazes a middle path between the modernist dichotomous dualism and postmodernist solipsistic monism. Nowhere in the Qur'ānic narrative is it suggested that there is no difference between the Qur'ānic Self and the Biblical Other – the respective identities of the two parties are alway relief. At the same time, the Qur'ān repeats over and over again, in different terms, from different perspectives and within different contexts that the Qur'ānic Self is intimately related with the Biblical Other (as well as Other Scriptural traditions).

In the Christian tradition, the Word becomes flesh in the person of Jesus Christ (peace be upon him); in the Muslim tradition the Revealed Word finds its ideal embodiment in the life and person of Muhammad (peace be upon him.) Consequently, the manner in which the Qur'ānic narrative deals with the issue of the Self and the Other should be reflected in the life of the Prophet. Of the numerous examples that his life provides for the practical illustration of the Self affirming itself through acknowledging and accepting the Other, perhaps none is more to the point than Muhammad's (peace be upon him) encounter with a delegation of Christians from Najran (a place in southern Arabia). This encounter took place in Medina, shortly after the Muslims had conquered Mecca and shortly before the Prophet's death. The account of this encounter, as recorded in the earliest of the biographies of the Prophet, is as follows:

Deputations still continued to come as in the previous year, and one of these was from the Christians of Najran, who sought to make a pact with the Prophet. They were of the Byzantine rite, and in the past had received rich subsidies from Constantinople. The delegates, sixty in number, were received by the Prophet in the Mosque, and when the time for their prayer came he allowed them to pray it there, which they did, facing towards the east.

At the audiences which they had with him during their stay, many points of his doctrine were touched on, and there were some disagreements between him and them concerning the person of Jesus. Then came the Revelation: 'Verily the likeness of Jesus with God is as the likeness of Adam. He created him of dust then said to him "Be!", and he was. This is the truth from thy Lord, so be not of the doubters. And whoso contendeth with thee about him after the knowledge that hath reached thee, say: Come ye, and let us summon our sons and your sons and our women and your women and ourselves and yourselves. Then we will imprecate, putting God's curse on those who lie.'[30]

The Prophet recited this Revelation to the Christians and invited them to meet with him and his family and to settle their dispute in the way here suggested. They said they would think about it, and the next day when they came to the Prophet they said that, 'Ali was with him, and behind them were Fatima and her two sons. The Prophet was wearing a large cloak and he now spread it wide enough to enfold them all in it, including himself. For this reason the five of them are reverently known as "the People of the Cloak". As to the Christians, they said they were not prepared to carry their disagreement so far as imprecation; and the Prophet made with them a favourable treaty according to which, in return for the payment of taxes, they were to have the full protection of the Islamic state for themselves and their churches and other possessions.'[31]

This description encapsulates the Qur'ānic ideal of the Muslim Self dealing with a non-Muslim Other. The Muslims receive the delegation of sixty Christians and the Muslim community as a whole acts as the host. Hospitality and ethical treatment of the stranger is part and parcel of Arab culture, and therefore not at all remarkable in the context of the present discussion. But what is remarkable about this encounter is that: 'The delegates, sixty in number, were received by the Prophet in the Mosque, and when the time for their prayer came he allowed them to pray it there, which they did, facing towards the east.' Other narrations state that 'when their time to pray came' refers to the Sunday Mass and the Eucharist. Above and beyond the expected and accepted levels of hospitality, the Prophet invites the Christians into Muslim sacred space to utilize the mosque for the Sunday services – an invitation that the Christians accept. In ethical terms, this is a postmodernist moment par excellence where all distinction between the Self and the Other is effaced.

While at the ethical level all difference between the Self and the Other is effaced, at the doctrinal level the difference is brought into such sharp relief that it comes to the very brink of a breaking point – the point of imprecation. This is a modernist moment par excellence where an unbridgeable divide between the Self and the Other is erected. The narrator observes that during the conversations between the Prophet and Christians 'many points of doctrine were touched on, and there were some disagreements between him and them concerning the person of Jesus'. Whereas this narration notes that a few *āyāt* were revealed addressing the 'points of doctrine' that were being discussed, other narrations suggest that approximately the first ninety *āyāt* of the third *sūra* were revealed during this particular 'Muslim–Christian dialogue'. This part of the Qur'ān throws into sharp relief the doctrinal differences between the Muslims and Christians, and provides the rationale behind these differences. In describing the differences in such stark terms, the Qur'ān delineates a sharp distinction between the Muslim Self and the Christian Other. It appears that the postmodernist moment of complete ethical inclusivity has been negated by the modernist moment of unbridgeable doctrinal exclusivity. But this is not in keeping with either the character of the Qur'ānic narrative, or the manner in which the Muslim–Christian encounter in Medina concluded.

The narrator observes that the Christians did not want to take the matter as far as imprecation and that 'the Prophet made with them a favourable treaty according to which, in return for the payment of taxes, they were to have the full protection of the Islamic state for themselves and their churches and other possessions'. In the final analysis, the Muslim Self and the Christian Other come to a mutual agreement and understanding that is acceptable to both parties and mutually beneficial terms of engagement and interaction are established. These terms are best described by the phrase 'relational duality' where the distinct and separate identity of the two parties is acknowledged by both, but at the same time the two parties are brought into mutually beneficial and mutually affirming relations. The terms of this agreement and the conclusion of this meeting demonstrate that it is not just the Muslim Self that is affirming itself by acknowledging and accepting the Other, the Christian Self is also affirming itself through the acknowledgement and acceptance of the Muslim Other.

The conclusion of the Muslim–Christian encounter in Medina should not be surprising in light of the basic ethos of the Qur'ānic narrative regarding the manner in which it addresses the issue of the Self and the Other. Beginning with the very first revelation bestowed upon Muhammad (peace be upon him) the Qur'ān as Revealed Self affirms itself by acknowledging and accepting the Written Other. Additionally, at the very beginning of its discourse (in terms of the arrangement of *sūras*) the Qur'ān as Scriptural Self affirms itself by acknowledging and accepting the Biblical Other. And finally in the life of the Prophet, in which the word finds its ideal embodiment, the Qur'ān as Muslim Self affirms itself by acknowledging and accepting the Non-Muslim Other. The logic of the Qur'ānic narrative makes possible a relationality between the Self and the Other that cannot be had from either the logic of modernist dichotomous dualism or postmodernist solipsistic monism. This is a relationality that makes possible living and enlivening relations among a variety of Selves – Selves that affirm themselves by accepting and embracing a variety of Others.

Scripture dialogue V: Space for the Other?

Jonah 3 and 4; al-Baqara (2) 62, Āl 'Imrān (3) 113-15

John 14.1-14; Āl 'Imrān (3) 19-20, 85

Both the Bible and the Qur'ān include texts which have been extensively appealed to by Christians and Muslims seeking answers to the pressing issue of how to account for, and how to respond to, people and communities of other faiths. In some cases, the relevance of a particular text to this issue may be apparent, though its accurate interpretation and contemporary implications may be more complex to determine. In other cases, a degree of ingenuity, in some cases even exegetical violence, must be used to extract a message pertinent to the issue. The tenor of the texts also varies to such an extent that some would speak of tensions on this question within the scriptural witness, while others would seek to identify a unified biblical or Qur'ānic teaching on issues of religious plurality, whether by harmonizing apparently disparate passages or by prioritizing some over others.

The texts which follow are in two groups. The former – two short passages from the second and third *sūras* of the Qur'ān and the second two chapters of the Book of Jonah – have been seen as emphasizing the universality of God's acceptance of people of differing religious backgrounds. The latter – two further passages from the third *sūra* and part of the fourteenth chapter of the Gospel of John – have by contrast often been appealed to in support of a narrower or harsher approach. All the texts belong together, however, in presenting Christians and Muslims with differing emphases as starting points for their reflections on this complex subject.

Biblical text: Jonah 3 and 4

3.1The word of the Lord came to Jonah a second time, saying, 2'Get up, go to Nineveh, that great city, and proclaim to it the message that I tell you.' 3So Jonah set out and went to Nineveh, according to the word of the Lord. Now Nineveh was an exceedingly large city, a three days' walk across. 4Jonah began to go into the city, going a day's walk. And he cried out, 'Forty days more, and Nineveh shall be overthrown!' 5And the people of Nineveh believed God; they proclaimed a fast, and everyone, great and small, put on sackcloth.

6When the news reached the king of Nineveh, he rose from his throne, removed his robe, covered himself with sackcloth, and sat in ashes. 7Then he had a proclamation made in Nineveh: 'By the decree of the king and his nobles: No human being or animal, no herd or flock, shall taste anything. They shall not feed, nor shall they drink water. 8Human beings and animals shall be covered with sackcloth, and they shall cry mightily to God. All shall turn from their evil ways and from the violence that is in their hands. 9Who knows? God may relent and change his mind; he may turn from his fierce anger, so that we do not perish.'

10When God saw what they did, how they turned from their evil ways, God changed his mind about the calamity that he had said he would bring upon them; and he did not do it.

4.1But this was very displeasing to Jonah, and he became angry. 2He prayed to the Lord, and said, 'O Lord! Is not this what I said while I was still in my own country? That is why I fled to Tarshish at the beginning; for I knew that you are a gracious God and merciful, slow to anger, and abounding in steadfast love, and ready to relent from punishing. 3And now, O Lord, please

120

take my life from me, for it is better for me to die than to live.' ⁴And the Lord said, 'Is it right for you to be angry?' ⁵Then Jonah went out of the city and sat down east of the city, and made a booth for himself there. He sat under it in the shade, waiting to see what would become of the city.

⁶The Lord God appointed a bush, and made it come up over Jonah, to give shade over his head, to save him from his discomfort; so Jonah was very happy about the bush. ⁷But when dawn came up the next day, God appointed a worm that attacked the bush, so that it withered. ⁸When the sun rose, God prepared a sultry east wind, and the sun beat down on the head of Jonah so that he was faint and asked that he might die. He said, 'It is better for me to die than to live.'

⁹But God said to Jonah, 'Is it right for you to be angry about the bush?' And he said, 'Yes, angry enough to die.' ¹⁰Then the Lord said, 'You are concerned about the bush, for which you did not labour and which you did not grow; it came into being in a night and perished in a night. ¹¹And should I not be concerned about Nineveh, that great city, in which there are more than a hundred and twenty thousand persons who do not know their right hand from their left, and also many animals?'

Notes on Jonah 3 and 4

3.2. Nineveh, the capital of the Assyrian empire, is remembered in the Hebrew Bible as a place bitterly hostile to, and destructive of, God's people Israel – the Book of Nahum has a fierce and gloating prophecy of its downfall. The unusual phrase used here to describe Nineveh's size literally translates 'God-almighty', and may be a first subtle pointer to the unexpected association of God with the city which the story unfolds.

3.5. The Ninevites 'believed God' – this does not mean that they became members of the covenanted people of Israel, but that they heeded the prophetic message and repented. This distinguishes them from the sailors of the first part of the story, who 'feared the Lord' (1.16 – note the difference of divine titles), and subsequently offered a sacrifice to Him.

The confession of divine mercy cited (with biting irony) by Jonah goes back to Exodus 34.6, where it indicates the Lord's forbearance towards his own people Israel – it is now their enemy Nineveh who is the recipient of mercy, much to Jonah's chagrin.

The titles 'Lord' [*Yhwh*] and 'God', previously distinguished in use according to whether the main human character is Jonah or the Ninevites, are in this verse first combined, and in the remainder of the chapter interchanged.

4.6-8. God makes a series of three divine 'appointments' from the natural world (a bush, a worm, a wind) to serve his purpose, following on from the 'appointment' of the fish to swallow Jonah in 1.17. These non-human creatures, like the non-Israelite people of Nineveh, prove more obedient to Him than the Israelite man appointed as a prophet.

Commentary on Jonah 3 and 4

These two chapters tell the second part of the story of Jonah, the prophet appointed by God to preach to Nineveh, the traditional enemy of Israel. In the first two chapters, Jonah has sought to evade God's plans by fleeing in the opposite direction, and suffered the indignity of being swallowed and vomited out by a fish. In these chapters, he proves equally recalcitrant, while the people of Nineveh, refusing to play the villainous part an Israelite readership would have expected of them, turn sincerely to God. The narrative probably dates from the post-exilic period, and can be seen (like the book of Ruth) as an affirmation of God's unrestricted concern for all people.

This message is persuasively and humorously conveyed through a text full of irony at different levels. While Jonah's acknowledgement of God's forgiving character is irony of a bitterly sarcastic kind, God's own humour – shown in the repeated inversion of expectations which he engineers – is of a much gentler kind. The prophet is led through his experiences to reflect on God's kindness and generosity, so graphically contrasted with his own vindictiveness, yet even this educational process is conducted with a light touch: uniquely, the book ends with the open horizon of a prophet being asked to ponder a question set by his God.

Alongside the reality of God's universal love for humanity, the narrative also stresses the universal possibility open to men and women of any nation to turn to that love in repentance. Indeed, the story hints that even non-human creatures can be seen as obediently serving the divine purpose. Although the end of the story brings together the two divine names 'Lord' (*Yhwh*) and 'God' (*Elōhîm*), in terms of human response a distinction can be drawn between, on the one hand, the explicit confession of the Lord, the God of Israel, and on the other the acknowledgement of the universal Creator. The former (to which some non-Israelites, such as the sailors of Jonah 1, may indeed be led) will involve participation in the Israelite cult, but the latter will manifest itself in contrition and moral amendment. It is this theme of a repentance open to all which will in turn provide the background for the theme of the 'sign of Jonah' as taught by Jesus in the Gospels.[32]

Qur'ānic texts: al-Baqara (2) 62; Āl 'Imrān (3) 113-15

2.62The believers, the Jews, the Christians and the Sabians – all those who believe in God and the Last Day and do good – will have their rewards with their Lord. No fear for them, nor will they grieve.

3.113But they are not all alike. There are some among the People of the Book who are upright, who recite God's revelations during the night, who bow down in worship, 114who believe in God and the Last Day, who order what is right and forbid what is wrong, who are quick to do good deeds. These people are among the righteous 115and they will not be denied (the reward) for whatever good deeds they do: God knows exactly who is mindful of Him.

Notes on al-Baqara (2) 62; Āl 'Imrān (3) 113-15

2.62. The identity of the 'Sabians', though much discussed by Muslim commentators, is unclear; this vagueness has meant that their position can be assigned to various groups of people, so that this verse has been used to support an open attitude towards religious plurality.

According to a statement attributed to the Prophet's cousin Ibn 'Abbās (d. 687), this verse – teaching that all who followed the path of their own prophets were accepted by God – was abrogated by 3.85 (see below), according to which from the time of Muhammad onwards only Islam was acceptable. However, this report and interpretation are rejected by others.

3.113. The division within the 'People of the Book' has been differently understood by later commentators. One reading sees here reference to the religious devotions of pious Christians and Jews. Others restrict this to those who have embraced Islam from a Jewish or Christian background, or who have adhered to the original 'pure' forms of these traditions – in which case the practices described are those followed by Muslims.

It is notable that the word used to describe those singled out for praise is *umma*, the expression commonly used for the Muslim community. In Muslim usage, the usual term for a non-Muslim religious community is *milla*.

114. 'Ordering what is right and forbidding what is wrong' is a characteristic duty of the Muslim community – cf. 3.104, where it is a contested question whether this is a responsibility laid on all Muslims or specifically on jurists. In this verse, it is associated with some from the 'People of the Book'.

Commentary on al-Baqara (2) 62; Āl 'Imrān (3) 113-15

Within *sūra al-Baqara*, which focuses on the Jewish people, verse 62 is placed following a description of divine punishments directed against the disobedient among the children of Israel. The point that divine disfavour is no respecter of an inherited religious identity is conveyed by a positive affirmation that divine favour reaches across religious boundaries. In *sūra Āl 'Imrān*, the main emphasis is on relations with Christians; verses 113-15 single out some Christians, Jews and other believers as especially worthy of praise. Both passages clearly teach, moreover, that the faithful people they are describing will be rewarded by God, and 2.62 shows that this is meant in an eschatological sense: they will have nothing to fear at the final Judgement.

These verses therefore seem to provide a firm basis within Islamic theology for a generous attitude towards at least some people of differing faiths, affirming that they will share with Muslims in the divine promise. It is true that the validity of such universalizing interpretations has been called into question in two ways by those who would adopt a narrower reading. One strategy is to identify the groups of people referred to in both verses either as Muslim converts from a Jewish or Christian background or as believers who have kept to an uncorrupted version of Judaism or Christianity – in which case, the religion which wins acceptance from God would be Islam rather than their original faiths.[33] The other is to see these verses as being abrogated by later passages which offer a narrower account of the scope of divine favour. While arguments between these differing views have been conducted on a textual level by appeals to differing parts of the *ḥadīth* literature, they also reflect the varying tenor of the relationships Muslims have had with the 'People of the Book', and with other non-Muslims, in various times and contexts.

Perhaps most notably, in sixteenth-century India, the Mughal emperor Akbar appealed to al-Baqara (2) 62 in seeking Qur'ānic support for his idea of a 'divine religion' *(dīn ilāhī)* within which all the varied faiths of his religiously diverse empire would be welcome.[34] Akbar's project, which failed rather quickly, involved extensive syncretism, and sought to extend the boundaries of divinely sanctioned faith and cult well beyond the monotheistic religions of the 'People of the Book'. However, with more sense of restraint, it has seemed plausible to some commentators to identify in both verses a common core of three principles – belief in the one true God, acknowledgement of a final moral accountability towards Him, and commitment to righteous action in obedience to Him in the present – which on an inclusive reading would constitute an authentic *dīn ilāhī* open to all and securing God's favour for all.

Biblical text: John 14.1-14

[1]'Do not let your hearts be troubled. Believe in God, believe also in me. [2]In my Father's house there are many dwelling places. If it were not so, would I have told you that I go to prepare a place for you? [3]And if I go and prepare a place for you, I will come again and will take you to myself, so that where I am, there you may be also. [4]And you know the way to the place where I am going.' [5]Thomas said to him, 'Lord, we do not know where you are going. How can we know the way?' [6]Jesus said to him, 'I am the way, and the truth, and the life. No one comes to the Father except through me. [7]If you know me, you will know my Father also. From now on you do know him and have seen him.'

[8]Philip said to him, 'Lord, show us the Father, and we will be satisfied.' [9]Jesus said to him, 'Have I been with you all this time, Philip, and you still do not know me? Whoever has seen me has seen the Father. How can you say, "Show us the Father"? [10]Do you not believe that I am in the Father and the Father is in me? The words that I say to you I do not speak on my own; but the Father who dwells in me does his works. [11]Believe me that I am in the Father and the Father is in me; but if you do not, then believe me because of the works themselves. [12]Very truly, I tell you, the one who believes in me will also do the works that I do and, in fact, will do greater works than these, because I am going to the Father. [13]I will do whatever you ask in my name, so that the Father may be glorified in the Son. [14]If in my name you ask me for anything, I will do it.'

Notes on John 14.1-14

1. The Greek *pisteuete*, occurring here twice, could on both occasions be translated either as an imperative ('Believe . . .') or as an indicative ('You believe . . .').

2. 'Dwelling place' is *monē*, which indicates a temporary lodging place on a journey.

6. The triplet of words 'the way, the truth, the life' is probably a Hebraism which should be interpreted as 'the true and living way'.

The mutuality of the Father-Son relationship in the Fourth Gospel is shown by the fact that this verse, announcing Jesus as the only way to the Father, is exactly balanced by 6.44, insisting that only the Father can 'draw' people to come to Jesus.

12. The opening words of the verse ('very truly') are literally 'Amen, Amen', a frequent formula in John to emphasize the gravity of what follows.

Commentary on John 14.1-14

This is part of the long speech of Jesus in John 13 – 17 known as the 'Farewell Discourse'. As the Lord takes leave of his disciples on the night of his being given up (which is also for John the path to his glory), the themes of travelling and of accompaniment are prominent. Jesus is journeying 'to the Father', and is preparing his friends for their own walking of the same road. The imagery here is rich and allusive; the horizon of the Lord's forthcoming death and resurrection is of course immediate, yet the passage also points to the eternally existing relationship of mutual indwelling between Father and Son which constitutes the life of God, and in which the disciples will themselves be guided through the gift of the Spirit. These chapters thus pick up the themes set out in the Prologue (1.1-14); as there the Word or self-communication of God is fully expressed through incarnation in a human person, so it follows here that the path that leads back to the Father should be through that same person. So it is that when Thomas asks to 'know the way' which he and his companions are to follow, Jesus responds that he is himself the living and true way which alone can guarantee access to the Father.

Thus the context makes clear that the famous verse 6 is in the first place addressed by Jesus to the disciples as guidance for his impending and their prospective journey. In contemporary pastoral liturgy, a resonance of this is appropriately found in the use of this passage in funeral services. Its more contested occurrence, however, is within debate about Christian attitudes to the salvation of people of other faiths, where it has often been used as a proof-text to support an 'exclusivist' position: if coming to the Father is only through the way of Jesus, it is claimed, then those who have not confessed Jesus as Lord cannot be saved. In fact, the harsh consequences of this kind of exclusivism will often be tempered in one way or another – by a countervailing emphasis on the divine will that 'all should be saved', or by a recognition that there may be ways or contexts unknown to us in which people may have a saving encounter with Jesus.

In a more systematic way, the exclusivist reading may itself be challenged by questioning the various assumptions which are bound up in its compressed line of argument. For example, a distinction might be made between 'coming to the Father' as a particularly intimate access to God made possible by Jesus and other, more broadly conceived, salvific ends.[35] Again, the exclusivist interpretation of John 14.6 is presented as a deductive argument from scripture which arrives at the conclusion that people other than Christians cannot come to the Father. A different approach would be to move inductively from the empirical 'evidence' of holiness in the lives of people of different faiths to conclude, on the basis of this same verse, that it must be by the way who is Jesus that these people are 'coming to the Father'.

While these and other possible interpretations take the verse in its present form as a starting point, still more radical approaches claim on the basis of historical-literary criticism that words like these cannot date back to the historical Jesus, and therefore can be safely dispensed with if they are problematic for formulating a Christian response to the religiously other. Whichever approach is adopted, and whatever the dangers of dealing with individual texts out of context, it seems likely that John 14.6 will continue to be a focus of contest for inter faith relations.

Qur'ānic texts: Āl 'Imrān (3).19-20, 85

[19]True Religion, in God's eyes, is total devotion (to Him alone). Those who were given the Scripture disagreed only out of rivalry, after they had been given knowledge – if anyone denies God's revelations, God is swift to take account – [20]if they argue with you (Prophet), say, 'I have devoted myself entirely to God and so have my followers.' Ask those who were given the Scripture, as well as those without one, 'Do you too devote yourselves to Him alone?' If they do, they will be guided, but if they turn away, your only duty is to convey the message. God is aware of His servants.

[85]If anyone seeks a religion other than complete devotion to God, his religion will not be accepted from him: he will be one of the losers in the Hereafter.

Notes on Āl 'Imrān (3) 19-20, 85

19. The 'rivalry' which has caused dissension among the People of the Book may be a reference to destructive divisions such as those which arose among the Christian churches regarding Christological and Trinitarian doctrine.

20. As the last sentence of the verse makes clear, the first person referred to in the speech here is the Prophet, pictured as engaging in disputation with recalcitrant members of the People of the Book.

'Those without a scripture' (*ummiyyīn*) are generally taken as the pagan Arab tribes of the Prophet Muhammad's time. The word used for these people is also used of the Prophet himself, who is believed to have received the Qur'ān in a state of being 'unlettered' (*ummī*).

The sense of the final sentence is to limit the responsibility of the Prophet: his task is to communicate the divine intention clearly, but not to direct or coerce the response of his hearers – a common theme in the Qur'ān (e.g. 5.99, 13.40, 24.54, 29.18, 36.17, 42.48) which parallels the thought of a biblical passage such as Ezekiel 33.

85. According to a (disputed) *ḥadīth* attributed through Ibn 'Abbās, this verse abrogates earlier, more seemingly generous passages such as 2.62 (see above). The one who will not 'accept' any religion other than Islam is here to be taken as God – this is a form of 'divine passive'.

Commentary on Āl 'Imrān (3) 19-20, 85

Both these passages appear on a first reading to state the categorical exclusion by God of all religions other than Islam as ways to winning divine acceptance. If moreover it is taken that these verses abrogate other Qur'ānic indicators (such as 2.62, see above) of a more inclusivist viewpoint, then it follows that the relation between Islam and other religions is to be seen theologically as simple and complete supersessionism. A strong consensus (*ijmā'*) to this effect has indeed traditionally existed among Muslims: 'The Jews, Christians, and the followers of all the religions, whether Zoroastrians, idol-worshippers or others, are all to be considered unbelievers as is specified in the Qur'ān and agreed upon by the Muslim community.'[36] Even if this exclusivist position is adopted, however, it does not necessarily entail the automatic damnation of any and all followers of non-Muslim religions. Islam teaches that the innate disposition (*fiṭra*) of humans is oriented towards a spontaneous monotheism unless and until distorted by subsequent misdirection, and in any case it emphasizes the sovereign mercy of God, which curtails prophetic responsibility for the response which any creature makes to the divine message.[37]

However, some Muslims would also wish to re-examine fundamentally the exclusivist consequences drawn from these texts, pointing in particular to two problems. One is the principle of abrogation (*naskh*) – that is, the replacement of one Qur'ānic text by another, considered to have been revealed later than that replaced. There are some widely accepted examples of this within the legal provisions of the scripture, and there are verses of the Qur'ān which can be read as supporting in principle the possibility of abrogation. However, the extension of abrogation to matters of faith regarding the hereafter is more strongly contested, and some scholars have felt more generally that the very idea of 'abrogation' is equivalent to 'falsification' or internal contradiction, which clearly cannot be applied to the Qur'ān.[38]

Secondly, within the text of both these passages there is a question about the interpretation of the word *'islām'*, described as that 'religion' (*dīn*) which is acceptable to God. While the 'exclusivist' (or, better, 'supersessionist') reading will identify this with the organized historical religion of Islam, as centred on the Qur'ān delivered by Muhammad, a more inclusive exegesis will see it as the obedient submission to God as Creator which is exemplified by the figure of Abraham, and which can be found as a heartfelt response from people of different religious communities. If *islām* can be understood in some such way as the primordial way of God open to all without the legal requirements involved in the acceptance of Islam as the historically constituted religion, then the tension between these verses and those (such as 2.62) of a more apparently inclusive tenor seems to be dissipated. However, this position probably remains at present a minority view within the Muslim community. What seems certain is that the interpretation of all the Qur'ānic material will continue to be a contested issue for Muslims facing issues of the religious Other.

Reflection 1: God, distinctive and universal

Both Christianity and Islam are challenged by the religious 'Other' – the person or community, whether (respectively) Muslim or Christian or of some other tradition – who follows a different path of faith. For both, that challenge raises questions about the nature and purposes of God as well as issues about the organization of religious life in society. As the scriptural texts show, the theological questions are most sharply posed in relation to the final destiny of the 'Other' – is he or she beyond the circle of divine acceptance, or can the Other in some way be seen to stand before God with the standing of the fellow believer? In much recent Christian theological writing, the rich variety of responses to this question of salvation have been classified under three broad types labelled as exclusivism ('only those who believe in Jesus Christ can be saved'), inclusivism ('all can be saved but only through Jesus Christ'), and pluralism ('all can be saved through their own religious paths') respectively.[39] However, any theology of the Qur'ānic passages which answers this question cannot be neatly fitted into one of these categories, but must include elements of each within a distinctive Islamic vision of the one God whose concern is universal. A growing body of Christian theological writing also is drawing attention to the limitations of the threefold schema, and likewise seeking a way of affirming a distinctive universality in God.[40]

So, all the passages of scripture discussed above could be described as conveying an 'exclusive' claim to truth in the sense that the God whom they understand to be universal is precisely the one to whom their faith bears witness, and no other. Nevertheless, even strongly exclusivist readings of particular scriptural verses have often held back from inferring that all outside the circle of faith will necessarily be lost, if this is seen to impugn the universal divine mercy. Again, both Christians and Muslims have also wanted to be 'inclusive' in giving an account from within their own understanding of faith that explains or involves the other. There are necessarily limits to this sense of inclusion too, though, as the account each gives of the other will certainly conflict at some points with the other's self-understanding: the differences of religious paths, and the conflicts of religious truth claims, are at some points irreducible. Finally, in the contemporary world the imperative of 'pluralism' cannot be avoided, when this is taken to be a serious recognition of the reality and integrity of other religious road maps to God and of the sincerity and coherence of other religious claims to truth. However, within both religious traditions there is a strong resistance to concluding from this the equality or equivalence of different faiths as vehicles of salvation. The challenge for both Christians and Muslims, then, seems to be to hold to the distinctive understanding of God revealed in and through their scriptures, and within the universality of that God's concern (which is part of his distinctiveness) to affirm a generous place for the Other.

Reflection 2: Religions, particular and universal

The challenge of the 'Other' is a social as well as a theological issue, as it involves different communities of faith finding ways to live alongside one another while maintaining their own integrity. There are long and varied histories of confronting this issue in societies where one or other faith has been dominant, or where they have been minorities with still others dominant. In Islamic history, a particular pattern of religious plurality was developed, which assured the civic pre-eminence of the Muslim community while guaranteeing freedom and security to Christians and other 'People of the Book'. In the West, a 'Christendom' model has generally been replaced by a broadly secular context which makes space for different religious groups on the basis of a shared commitment to human rights – though this need not preclude recognition of a particular place in public life for one or other branch of the Christian Church. In the case of any pattern of social organization, it is needful for Christians and Muslims to interrogate the theological and philosophical basis on which 'pluralism' is predicated and organized, and to evaluate this not only in terms of their own faith but also with a concern to safeguard the religious freedom of others, especially minorities.

All our thinking about the place of God-ward faith, and the diversity of God-ward faith, in society is hampered by the inadequacies of the term 'religion' and the excessively institutional associations that word so often carries today.[41] It is striking that both Christian and Islamic scriptures speak in more fluid and responsive terms of a 'way' or 'path' which constitutes the human response to God. The Qur'ānic term *dīn* also seems to point to a fuller sense of 'religion' which can express an optimal answer made by individuals and communities to the divine invitation. inter faith dialogue, and inter-scriptural exegesis, can build on a recognition of both the diversity and the commonality of this response to create an attitude of appreciation for the other in the fullness of their own *dīn*. This involves us in going beyond tolerance – one definition of which is 'the power, constitutional or acquired, of enduring poison'[42] – to build up a culture which is more truly pluralist and more respectful of one another.

Christian theology and other faiths

Rowan Williams

Imagine you are looking up some statistics about an African country – population, main exports, ethnic groupings and so on; there will probably be an entry for 'religions', and it may read like this – 'Muslims 40%, Christians 38%, Hindus 3%, traditional religions 19%'. It looks very straightforward, rather like a run-down of political allegiances or tribal distribution. It is one defining activity or characteristic among others. But one thing I want to suggest here is that it is the sort of formula that can suggest significant misunderstanding, a misunderstanding that affects both popular thinking and public policy in our own country; and I think we need a bit of theology to help us to a more sensible position.

So what is actually wrong with this breakdown of religious loyalties? The problem is roughly this. We Westerners tend to think that a 'religion' is a distinct system of ideas, beliefs that connect the world as we see it with a whole lot of non-visible powers or realities, which have to be paid attention to, worshipped or at least negotiated with, in order to have the maximum security in life. Religions express themselves in beliefs but also in distinctive practices like periods of self-denial, meetings for ritual actions and festivals. So far so good, in one sense. The dangerous assumption follows, though, that the world as we see it is pretty clear; we can agree about it – whereas the powers that religion tries to connect with are invisible, so that we cannot expect to agree about them. What they have in common is claims that cannot be proved by appealing to the world as we all see it. So a Christian, a Muslim, a Buddhist and a Ghanaian or Papuan villager performing rituals handed down from time immemorial are all performing variations of the same thing; and that same thing is always set over against the obvious, 'public', shared world of what we can see. Life divides between things that are common to everyone and things that are unclear and therefore do not belong in the public and everyday. What 'religion' you belong to is simply a matter of which set of beliefs you happen to entertain in that bit of your life which is left over for this kind of thing.

But when we try to talk with the Muslim or the villager in particular, things get to look more complicated. The villager will undoubtedly say that performing rituals is as routine and necessary and uncontroversial a thing as milking cows; indeed, it may well be that the way you milk cows is dictated by rituals that seem to the outsider to have not very much to do with cows as we see them. Dylan Thomas memorably quotes in the preface to his 'Collected Poems' the Welsh shepherd who was asked why he still performed rituals in fairy rings to protect his sheep; he replied (doubtless with scorn for the silliness of the question), 'I'd be a damn fool if I didn't.' There just is not an ordinary world from which this villager takes time off to practise his 'traditional religion'. The same with the Muslim, in a more sophisticated way: the ordinary day you have to get through is marked in time intervals every bit as natural or obvious as the hours of the clock to us, the intervals between the five prayer times. There is no neutral time that needs interrupting to do religious things: the ordinary is the religious.

And just to take one more example of possible confusion: Buddhists have festivals and temples and statues, so they are obviously people who do this religious thing. But what are the invisible forces they deal with? For the strictest southern Buddhist at least, though in one sense for all Buddhists, the invisible forces are inside us; doing 'religious' things is not a matter of how to negotiate with an invisible world outside us at all, but of learning an all-inclusive set of mental habits that gradually changes the way you relate to this world and frees you from inner suffering and frustration.

So my imaginary African country cannot after all be split up into four neat segments of religious belief, four varieties of one thing, that thing being a set of more or less chosen beliefs about invisible states of affairs alongside the ordinary world. What we have instead is rather a variety of styles of living, each of which has a very different account of the world as a whole, life as a whole. And although this may be rather obvious when you think about it, it does have some far-reaching consequences. Think for a moment about the old Indian parable of the blind men and the elephant – one grasps its tail and says, 'It's a rope', one grasps its leg and says 'It's a tree', and so on. This is often used as a way of saying that we can never really tell the truth in religious matters, we all see things only from a limited perspective and so on. But we are missing the point; someone knows it is an elephant, and the force of the metaphor is not so much that no one can know what the invisible sacred reality is actually like as that we are all painfully capable of reaching for the easiest language, the language that fits our own individual experience, when speaking of God, and fail to compare notes with each other or to submit what we say to an acknowledgement that the scale of what we are talking about should teach us some caution. The one thing the parable is not really about is a distinction between what everyone can see and what some people unreasonably argue about.

Now this is where theology begins to come into the picture. The model that draws all those very different kinds of life together as varieties of one thing called religion assumes, as I have said, that there is an open space in which people can meet when they're not being religious. When public policy documents talk about involving faith communities in this or that piece of social regeneration, the assumption is likewise that these particular special interest groups can all be harnessed to doing useful work in the open public space, where their disagreements can be buried for a while; they can be persuaded to cooperate in working with what everybody sees, what no one argues over. I do not deny that there is something in this, and I will come back to it later. But theology, the religious use of the mind, whether Christian or not, is going to start from somewhere else.

Religious language talks about the entire environment in terms of its relation with the holy. As Wittgenstein said, it is more like talking about colour – something that affects everything (literally) in sight – than talking about an item in a list of things. Theology, the work of religious intellect, tries to work out what the implications are of seeing everything in relation to a holy reality that is never absent. It is not about advice as to what we should do when in the territory marked off as religious, where we do business with invisible rather than visible things; it is about what lives should look like when they find their meaning as a whole in relation to holy reality. To put it a bit differently, theology tries to make connections between the stories told about the holy or the fundamentally real and the words and actions people use in order to let those stories take hold of their lives and give them shape in every detail and aspect.

I know the difficulties in using 'theology' to describe certain Muslim or Jewish, let alone Buddhist intellectual activities; the word feels most at home in a Christian context. But every tradition of faith has a tradition of reflecting on the normal words and acts that make up a life of faith. Jews, Christians and Muslims all connect this with reflection on holy books, sorting out the consistency of passages that do not immediately seem consistent, settling what are agreed to be the implications of a story or a formula or a rule. Buddhists likewise use a set of holy texts, but, in some Buddhist traditions at least, are interested in working out the implications for how we think about knowledge and language of the basic instructions given to help us purge our minds of greed and fantasy. So I recognize that in implying that 'theology' can cover all of this, I may be pushing things rather; but my basic point is that all religious practices go along with habits of disciplined thinking, exploring interrelated ideas or metaphors, making connections and searching for consistencies. Even where practice is what we unhelpfully call 'primitive', reflection goes on, sometimes in the generation of new stories; mythology often reflects ways of solving problems or suggesting connections by storytelling. If in Greek myth Athena springs fully-armed from the head of Zeus, this encodes a recognition that wisdom or the sense of order is completely contained in and intimately related to the source of creative power; and that is a 'theological' point. Ultimate power cannot be stupid; wisdom cannot be just a lucky human guess.

So as reflection matures and more connections are made, what comes to light is a map of how things are on which people attempt to 'plot' human behaviour. And what this means is that disagreements between religious traditions are very significantly disagreements about the kind of universe we inhabit, what that universe makes possible for human beings; and what is the most truthful or adequate or even sane way of behaving in the universe. The passion in religious disagreement comes not simply from abstract differences as to how the holy is to be talked about, but from differences as to how human life is to be lived so as to be in fullest accord with 'the grain of the universe'. A different view on this means a life lived less fully in accord with truth, and so a life deprived of significant happiness. Inevitably, then, the disagreements are profound; to the extent that a religious tradition has the generous belief that it is given something of health-giving relevance for all human beings, it will be strong in its arguments with other traditions.

This may at first sound an unwelcome approach. But I think it is of enormous importance to see why religious disagreement is serious, and why it cannot be reduced to that realm of essentially private difference, outside the clear light of neutral day, where modern secular society is comfortable leaving it. And what I am going to try and argue is that once we are clearer about the nature and scope of religious disagreement, we are actually more rather than less likely to develop a respectful and collaborative practice in inter faith relations.

This has something to do with the fact that when we see our differences as theological in the sense I have outlined, as differences about what a fully meaningful, sane or truth-revealing life looks like in the light of convictions about the universe itself and its source, we begin to see that not all religious claims are answers to the same questions. If, say, Islam and Christianity were two sets of solutions to one problem, their relation would be one of simple rivalry, systematic mutual exclusion. But in fact the two faiths work with importantly different accounts of creation and humanity. It will not do to say either that they are essentially the same or that they are utterly incompatible. What needs to be avoided is, for example, a Christian approach which says simply that Islam is a failed solution to the question satisfactorily answered by Christianity.

The difficulties of such an approach appear most clearly when we look at Christian–Jewish relations. The appalling history here is in large part the result of a Christian claim to be the correct answer to a question wrongly answered by Jewish faith and practice – 'Who is the Messiah?' As a great deal of modern scholarship makes clear, the greater part of Jewish reflection, 'theology' if you will, for two thousand years has not begun from any such question. For the Jew to be told that in Christian eyes he or she has wrongly answered a question either not asked or asked in a wholly different context is in effect for the Jew to be told that there is no fundamental difference between them and the Christian; the Christian way of talking has included the Jew, quite irrespective of what the Jew is actually saying.

Similarly with Islam, where the Christian may sometimes feel a bit like the Jew in the preceding paragraph. In the light of the witness of

Muhammad as the seal of prophetic revelation, all previous history, including that of Jesus, comes together in a single pattern. If the question is 'What is the climax of prophecy, where in divine word and human example is the will of God most completely made known?' the Muslim naturally answers in terms of the Qur'ān and the Prophet; the Christian has to struggle to explain that the unique relation of Jesus to God and the incorporation of Christian believers into that relation are beliefs that connect with different questions and need a different narrative structure. A conversation some years ago with an articulate and evangelistic Muslim taxi driver has left a deep impression on me in this regard: it was very clear to him that the mere fact of Islam having appeared later than Christianity provided a powerful case for Christians to change their frame of reference. It should be obvious that here at last was the hitherto unrevealed end of the story. To be a Christian was to leave the theatre at the interval.

So quite a bit of interreligious encounter, historically and at the casual level, tends to settle for this basic idea, that the representative of another faith is really, as it were, speaking the same language but making appalling mistakes which render proper communication in the language impossible. I could multiply examples, but let me just mention in passing the implication, for a Westerner, of calling Buddhism 'atheistic'; the same kind of problem. A properly theological approach, I suggest, is one in which we first try to clarify what question it is to which my own religious language seeks to give answers, and so to engage with other traditions in relation to what their fundamental questions are. And when we come to consider the truth of religious statements, at least we shall not be trapped into seeing this as a process of comparing a series of answers in a kind of examination.

But what does this say about religious truth? There is no vantage point above all traditions and theologies from which some completely detached person can decide; no board of examiners. But this also means that there is no perspective from which someone can say, 'These are all different ways of looking at the same material.' If I am a person of faith, a person whose life is lived in a comprehensive relationship with what I understand to be the source and context of all life, I cannot appeal to someone out there in the neutral public world to provide me with credentials. So I do not think that religious relativism or pluralism will do, as this seems always to presuppose the detached observer (the one who sees the whole elephant); but neither can we expect to find a tribunal to assess right and wrong answers.

Yet our traditions claim to be true, and, just as importantly, to be about how lives are to be led that are in accord with how the universe is; they are about happiness as well as truth, or rather, they are about truthfulness as the condition of happiness and happiness as the fruit of truthfulness. They do not simply claim to give a correct description of the world in relation to holy reality, they sketch in greater or lesser detail how that relation is to be made specific in daily practice, so that each human life is shaped into an appropriate response. Such response may be characterized as covenantal obedience, self-sacrifice, self-dissolution or whatever else, depending on the basic story told about the universe and its source. But how do we get to assessments of truth from such a perspective?

The question is raised in its most sensitive and painful form by the phenomenon of conversion. Very often, when people move from one religious tradition to another, when they recognize a fuller or more final truth in another language and practice of faith, it is because of a sense that the universe portrayed in this other tradition is a more full or resourceful environment, or that the humanity imagined here is one with greater possibilities and beauties. But this only happens when someone begins to experience the world differently – not simply when a new set of ideas is presented. Sharing a different sort of life makes all of us wonder about the questions and answers we have taken for granted; they may seem misconceived or even subtly oppressive. A different tradition is attractive when it makes you think that this is the all-important question you have never asked, so that this kind of life now appears as transparent to a greater truth. It is not that a person suddenly sees the right answer to a question that has previously been wrongly answered, but that the new world exposes a whole frame of reference as somehow inadequate.

And change from one tradition to another is painful for your former fellow-believers precisely because there is an implied judgement on a whole life, a whole language. Its positive effect, though, ought always to be a deeper self-critical understanding of why someone might find this tradition too limiting to inhabit, an urgency about exploring the resources given. The point I am moving to, however, is that the 'contest' over religious truth happens most effectively and authentically when a real sharing of worlds is possible. And that in turn happens only when we do not live in a social order that totally controls the possibilities of experiencing the Other. To this extent, the modern revolt against theocracy, against the religious control of social options, is justified. But I think that the implication is actually the opposite of what is usually thought. We are used, as I said at the beginning, to thinking of the modern social space as one in which it is impossible to have any very meaningful talk about religious truth because there is a neutral public arena in which truth can be argued about and a private area of commitment to unprovable beliefs. But in fact a non-theocratic society allows real contention about religious truth by the mere fact of giving space for different experiences and constructions of the universe to engage with each other, to be themselves.

This is the practical outworking of my earlier point that when we see our differences as theological we may have better and more collaborative relations. If religious faith is not just a set of private beliefs about supernatural things but a comprehensive ground for reflection on how the world and human life hang together, then to establish the truth of any set of religious claims must be a form of showing that this sort of religious language rather than another has the resource to hold together the greatest spread of human experience. There can be no final and unanswerable mode of establishing this by argument. We can only ask if there could ever be convergence about the character of the world and humanity such that we could better see the 'fit' of certain words or images. In that sense, the awareness in modern culture of the plurality of religious practice is a positive matter. We have become more aware of the range of what any religious talk has to cope with, the cultural variety, the historical reach, the challenges in catastrophe, pain and tragedy to certain kinds of claim. The point was expressed poignantly by Simone Weil when she said that an indigenous American who had lived through the genocidal terror of the age of the Conquistadors, who had seen massacre and plague and the destruction of a culture, might or might not retain an allegiance to their 'traditional religion'; but if they did, they would nonetheless think differently about the holy from any thoughts they could have had before. It is an insight taken up by a good many indigenous peoples in our own age. Perhaps one could also point to something similar in the crises and agonies of modern Jewish thought. In the fiction of Isaac Singer – to take only one example – we read about the 'timeless' world of faith in the *shtetl*, the East European Jewish village, with its piety, its folklore, its proverbial wisdom and petty folly, its absolute spiritual solidity; and we read about the lives of rootless post-war emigrés, happy neither in the USA nor in Israel, trying to understand what the truth of their Jewish identity and loyalty means in the wake of the most nightmarish disruption imaginable. If that truth can be vindicated in the 'new world' after the camps, its truth claims must be taken more seriously and understood more deeply.

And thus what we come to see in each other as religious communities in the context of the variegated world of modernity, of 'global' society, is a range of behaviours each of which seeks to understand how it is to include, to 'narrate' (if I can use a fashionable term), the whole range of a world which is no longer the property of any one of them. This does not mean that every religious tradition seeks to adjust and accommodate itself to modernity or that truth is reduced to the capacity to cope with global culture without tears. Far from it: each will, if it knows its business, sharpen its critique of the myths of secular neutrality, each will seek to show how it can contain and effectively transform the particular challenges to its account of humanity thrown up by the new environment; each will struggle to show that it is not reduced to impotence by the complexity of modern discourse. So, although the pressure of modernity may often produce a powerfully reactionary strategy in some religious believers, the sort of thing we generically and not very helpfully call fundamentalism, the pressure is also visible to demonstrate how a tradition in its full integrity can make intelligible order of the chaos around by extending and renewing its repertoire of image and concept. We could think of the history of the Brahma Samaj in India, of the Sufi-influenced Western Islamic apologetic of writers like Gai Eaton or Martin Lings, or of the revival of Russian Orthodox social and philosophical energy at both the beginning and the end of the twentieth century.

Seeing each other like this in the non-confessional, non-theocratic state and culture of modernity, we are better able to avoid the errors I mentioned earlier, the errors that arise from supposing that other faiths have bad answers to the questions for which you have good answers. The issue is now how we exhibit in practice the claims we all in different ways make about our tradition's ability to tell a truth which will comprehend any human situation it may encounter. Precisely because this is a complex, humanly unpredictable business, in which none of us is going to be able to pronounce a final conclusion acceptable to all, precisely because this is not in any ordinary sense a competition with winners and losers, we need time and space for it. And such time and space are in principle given in societies that assume religious freedom as fundamental, that do not close down the variegated possibilities of the modern. If we start retreating to theocracy, we are by implication admitting that our religious tradition cannot sustain itself in a complex environment; states (Christian, Muslim or Hindu) that enact anti-conversion laws or penalize minority faith groups may have an understandable wish to resist unfair pressure or manipulation in proselytizing, but they confess a profound and very disturbing lack of confidence in their own religious resourcefulness.

This is one reason why I see no problem in the fostering of faith schools of different complexions in our own country. Christian faith is no longer legally protected here as the only legitimate religious activity; but the existence of church schools forces Christians to engage actively with public life, with how society forms its new generations. It forces Christians, you could say, to try to be credible, professional, articulate, in the public arena. Similar partnerships between statutory authority and other religious communities should have the effect of drawing those communities into public conversation, pressing them to become publicly credible in new ways. And this must be healthy for both society at large and the communities in question, since it ought to be the opposite of ghettoization. It educates faith communities as it educates the managers of our educational systems, and it obliges us to take each other more seriously as faith communities.

Significant inter faith encounter arises from our being able to see each other doing whatever it is we do as well as possible – teaching, worshipping, reflecting, serving. For me, one of the most important such encounters I have ever had was this spring in Qatar, when I was part of an international group of Muslims and Christians meeting to read their scriptures together and discuss them; we Christians were able to benefit enormously from watching Muslims doing what Muslims do with love, intellectual rigour and excitement. It proved a deeper and more truly respectful meeting of minds than any attempt to find a neutral common ground. We met as theologians, committed to exploring the reality of what truthful and holy lives might look like and how they might be talked about. And so we were able not to see each other as competing to answer the same exam paper. At times there was deep convergence, at times monumental disagreement. But I suspect we all emerged with a sharper sense of what our traditions had to deal with, of the complexity of our world and the difference of our questions. My hope for the future of dialogue is for more such exchanges at every level.

But I want to turn in conclusion to two specific issues, at which I have already hinted. I want briefly to say something about the general relation of faith communities to the wider society; and I want to add a few reflections specifically as a Christian theologian on the ideas sketched here. On the first issue: it is true that faith communities have something in common over against a secular frame of reference. They all have disciplines of examining the honesty and consistency of believers, ways of encouraging self-scrutiny; they all assume that we are likely to be deceived about ourselves for quite a bit of the time. They all assume that what we are finally answerable to is something other than just the majority vote in a society at any one time. They all teach us to look critically at what seem to be our instinctive choices, and they all warn us against thinking that the material environment (including the human body) is just there to serve such instinctive human choices. There is a basis for what some like to call a 'global ethic' in all this, even if it is primarily negative rather than positive.

However, when there are attempts by governments or international agencies to harness this in support of this or that programme for human improvement, it is important that there should not be misunderstanding. Sometimes there can be an expectation that religious communities will simply follow a broadly liberal social agenda, and a consequent anger and disappointment when this does not materialize. This may be when Islamic and Roman Catholic bodies join to resist a programme which assumes that abortion is a naturally just means of population control; when Christians and Hindus join in objecting to genetically modified crops in Asia; when Muslims condemn globalization because of its dependence on un-Islamic means of handling money through interest and speculation; when people of a wide variety of religious commitments unite to challenge embryo research. All these issues are complex, and my point is not to suggest that there is a single religious 'line' on any of them. What matters is to recognize that the religious person or group starts from a perspective which on some questions will deliver conclusions similar to those of the secular progressive, and on some questions most definitely will not. The secular progressive tends to think it is a happy chance that makes religious folk agree with the self-evident goals of human justice and welfare. If we are to avoid deep anger, frustration and anti-religious animus, it is important for the secularist to acknowledge that they may find themselves working alongside religious believers who look to the same goals for radically different reasons; and thus to recognize that the goals of secular justice are not after all so self-evident. One of the most important tasks of religion in our culture, I dare to say, is to challenge the secularist to produce good and coherent grounds for their goals. And this is made all the harder by the assumption I have been challenging – that 'religion' is a subdivision of human activity which belongs among the optional extras, after you have attended to the clear imperatives of non-religious public life. The secular assumption too must strive to make itself credible; when it refuses this, we have a mirror image of theocracy – an uncriticized ideology defining the terms of public life. This is why the partnership between faith communities and public agencies, as in education, is good for both.

And finally: where would I put Christian theology on the sort of map I have been outlining? Christian theology says that the world exists because of the utterly free decision of a holy power that is more like personal life than anything else; that we can truthfully speak of as if it had mind and will. It says that the purpose of this creation is that what is brought into being from nothing should come to share as fully as possible in the abundant and joyful life of the maker. For intelligent beings, this involves exercising freedom – so that the possibility is there of frustrating one's own nature by wrong and destructive choices. The purpose of God to share the divine life is so strong, however, that God acts to limit the effects of this destructiveness and to introduce into creation the possibility of an intensified relation with the divine through the events of the life of Jesus of Nazareth, above all in his sacrificial death. This new relation, realized by the Spirit of God released in Jesus' rising from the grave, is available in the life of the community that gathers to open itself to God's gift by recalling Jesus and listening to the God-directed texts which witness to this history.

So what matters for the Christian? That the world is for joy and contemplation before it is for use (because it comes from God's freedom and delight, not to serve the purpose of a selfish divine ego); that our account of our own human nature and its needs is dangerously fallible and that we are more limited than we can know in our self-understanding; that it is God's gift in a particular and unique set of events in the world that it becomes possible for us to be released from some of the most lethal effects of this fallibility; and that the new possibility is bound in with life in community centred on praise and listening and mutual nurture. This is the Christian universe in (very) small space. It must argue against other traditions that the world comes from and as deliberate gift (Buddhists would disagree), that our self-deception is so radical and deep-seated that we cannot be healed by the revelation of divine wisdom and law alone (Jews and Muslims would disagree), that our healing is a 'remaking' effected through a once and for all set of events (Muslims and Hindus would disagree). The Christian must argue that because this picture of the universe makes the fullest allowance possible for human failure and self-deceit and gives the most drastic account possible of divine presence in addressing this failure (God coming to inhabit creation in Jesus), it has a good claim to comprehensiveness as a view of how things are. But it is assailed by those who say that its doctrines of original sin are self-indulgent excuses for the weakness of the will, that its concentration on history limits it to parochial perspectives or ties it to a remote and disputed past, that its view of the common life is weak and fails to make the necessary bid for social transformation in a comprehensive way (a particularly strong Muslim point).

And meanwhile, the Christian is struck and challenged by the fact that outside the visible fellowship of faith, lives are lived which look as though they are in harmony with the Christian universe – which give the right place to contemplation and joy, to self-forgetfulness and the awareness of gift. The theological task is not only to go on patiently clarifying the implications of the Christian universe and reflecting on the sort of critiques I have sketched, but also to think about how such lives outside the frame are made possible and sustained. There is no quick answer to this, certainly no answer that would justify us in saying, 'Forget the doctrine, all that matters is the practice', since the doctrine is what nourishes and makes sense of the practice. Our doctrine is still in formation; and the question of how holy lives can exist outside our own tradition has throughout Christian history led to some of the most searching and far-reaching extensions of our language about the significance of Jesus. I trust that this will go on being the fruit of such questioning. But my aim here has been primarily to plead for our dialogue to take place at the level of how we place ourselves in the whole universe of our systems, and how we imagine lives that are holy, that are in the fullest sense 'natural', in accord with how things are. At this level, we do not see others either as bad or unsuccessful copies of ourselves or as people who have a few casual variants on a single shared truth. We have to see how very other our universes are; and only then do we find dialogue a surprise and a joy as we also discover where and how we can still talk about what matters most – holiness, being at peace with what most truly is.

Chapter 5
Scriptures in dialogue

The Qatar seminar was distinctive in building its dialogue around the joint reading by Christians and Muslims of passages from the Bible and the Qur'ān. Held at a time when dramatic events in the region were impinging on Muslim–Christian relations globally – coalition troops were entering Baghdad at the time of the meeting in Doha – this way of dialogue through engagement with scripture made deep sense. For Muslims and for Christians, the scriptures are central to identity, beliefs, ethics, worship and ways of living. As great changes affect our world and our communities, there is an urgent need continually to remember, study and interpret these formative texts in order to be faithful to God in new circumstances. Christianity and Islam both have long traditions of scriptural understanding, and many ways of developing these traditions further to meet new situations and questions. But there are almost no places and occasions where Christians and Muslims can learn from each other and engage in dialogue around the scriptures together. It is also sadly true that many of the most disturbing things that happen in the name of Islam and Christianity are justified by reference to the Qur'ān and the Bible. Any progress towards deeper understanding and peacemaking between the two faiths must, therefore, take these scriptures seriously, because they are linked to the best and the worst in history and in the current situation.

The textually based method shaped the pattern and the character of the dialogue in Qatar. With scripture at the centre of reflection, discussion and deliberation, it was the scriptural narrative that identified the parameters within which particular issues and concerns were discussed. In contrast to some other modes of inter faith discussion, where scripture may be almost incidental to the discussion, or be brought in only sporadically and haphazardly, one participant observed that here it felt that it was the living breath of the revealed Word that was the moving spirit behind the discussion, rather than abstract conceptual constructs of academic or theological discourse. Once the scriptures were opened and read, he said, an air of familiarity seemed to pervade the room; a peaceful and trustful atmosphere emerged, seemingly out of nowhere. It was this sense of shared intellectual and spiritual striving in response to the Word which made it possible for Christians and

Muslims together to address some pointed and difficult issues in forceful yet positive discussions. As our scriptures permeate our lives, so listening to each other grappling with texts offered us all a glimpse of each other's hearts as well as minds.

It was notable that a dialogue based around scripture led as much into the exploration of differences as into the identification of common ground. This was even true of passages which at first appeared to share a common focus – those relating to Abraham, for example. More generally, in both scriptures we found passages which are 'inclusive', in the sense that they show God's universal purposes, but in both also we met more demanding passages, which emphasize the need for response to a specific revelation and the threat of judgement to those who proved faithless.

Differences are also apparent at a methodological level, in the ways in which Christians and Muslims approach their respective scriptures, and at a theological level, in the ways in which they receive them as conveying the divine Word. It is clear that, by and large, Muslims and Christians view the inspiration of scripture in very different ways. For the one, it is possible to take account of the history of a text's transmission (including its background in oral tradition) as well as its later redaction, and at the same time to hold to the text's inspired status. For the other, divine inspiration is understood more directly and precludes literary and historical considerations regarding the text of scripture, even if other elements in the tradition are not exempt from such study.

Reading scripture in the company of the Other underlines the importance of a certain humility in exegesis. It reminds the reader that there are many things in his or her 'own' scripture which he or she will never fully or definitively comprehend. The Bible and the Qur'ān speak to Christians and Muslims as texts which are full of meaning at many different levels, and as texts whose meaning will elude them at many levels also. The Qur'ān affirms of itself that it includes 'ambiguous' verses whose import is known only to God. Augustine describes the Bible as a great and high room, but with a door so low that one must stoop in humility to enter into it. In an age when many in both faiths brush aside the very possibility of any uncertainty in their interpretation of scriptural truth, this lesson of exegetical humility is a valuable one for us to learn from one another. None of us has, and none of us ever will have, explored all the riches of our scriptures.

There is clearly ample scope for further engagement of Christians and Muslims together in a dialogue grounded in their reading of the scriptures together. One long and pressing agenda for such a dialogue is set for us by the massive transformations of recent centuries. This is especially obvious in relation to gender issues, but in other ways too dialogue cannot be only with one another (and with people of other religions); it must also engage with the secular understandings and forces in our religious and secular world. Guided by their engagement with the scriptures, Muslims and Christians face the challenge of discerning together what in these tendencies is to be affirmed, what rejected, and what reformed. Nevertheless, the greatest 'issue' which draws us into dialogue must be the reality of God and the seeking of his will for our world. Unclear as the way ahead may be, it does seem to be God's purpose that Muslims and Christians should continue to follow through a dialogue of truth-seeking and peace-making. It is for the sake of God, and in line with God's will and wisdom, that we come together to engage in study of scriptures together. Each of us love our scriptures above all as writings through which God is revealed. As one participant at the Qatar seminar said, 'Long-term devotion to God is the best context for understanding our scriptures.'

The beginning of the twenty-first century is a time when there is an urgent need for Christians and Muslims to engage with each other more deeply for the sake of understanding, peace-making, the blessing of the world, and the glorifying of God, and also a time when there are unprecedented conditions and opportunities for such engagement. We have found in the Qur'ān and the Bible texts that can sustain us in a deep and searching dialogue with one another. The challenge facing us now is to develop ways of continuing this in the future so that each of our traditions and all of our societies can be shaped by the wisdom to be gained from our scriptures.

Notes

Chapter 2   Listening to God, learning from scripture

1. Luke 9.31.
2. Luke 9.22; 13.33; 15.32; 17.25; 22.37; 24.7, 26, 44.
3. Luke 24.21.
4. Luke 24.25–7.
5. Luke 24.44–7.
6. Luke 24.47.
7. Acts 17.7.
8. Tom Wright, *The New Testament and the People of God*, London: SPCK, 1992 and *Jesus and the Victory of God*, London: SPCK, 1996.
9. Matthew 28.18.
10. Luke 24.35.
11. Luke 24.49.
12. Other Christian traditions of course have similar patterns; I write of those with which I am familiar.
13. As quoted in C. Brown (ed.), *Dictionary of New Testament Theology*, Exeter: Paternoster, 1975, vol. 1, p. 7.
14. Luke 24.31.
15. Genesis 3.7.
16. We are witnessing in our day a healthy reawakening of interest in imagination as an important part of Christian and human life; it is perhaps important not to draw too heavy a borderline between imagination and prayer.
17. al-Baqara (2) 285.
18. al-Nūr (24) 51.
19. al-Anfāl (8) 21.
20. al-Jāthiya (45) 8.
21. al-Ḥajj (22) 46.
22. al-Aḥqāf (46) 30.
23. al-Qaṣaṣ (28) 36.
24. See, for example, Khaled Abou El Fadl, *Speaking in God's Name: Islamic Law, Authority and Women*, Oxford: Oneworld, 2001, esp. pp. 141–208.
25. al-Raʿd (13) 39.
26. al-Tawba (9) 6.
27. Ibn ʿArabī's approach to the Qurʾān is discussed in Michael Chodkiewicz, *An Ocean Without Shore: Ibn ʿArabī's, the Book, and the Law*, tr. David Streight, Albany, NY: SUNY Press, 1993.
28. Āl ʿImrān (3) 7.
29. Ṣād (38) 8.
30. al-Anʿām (6) 75-79.
31. al-Naḥl (27) 16.

32. Peirce defined the index as 'a sign, or representation, which refers to its object not so much because it is associated with general characters which that object happens to possess, as because it is in dynamical (including spatial) connection both with the individual object, on the one hand, and with the sense or memory of the person for whom it serves as a sign, on the other hand'. See Justus Buchler (ed.), *The Philosophy of Peirce, Selected Writings*, London: Routledge & Kegan Paul, 1956, p. 107.

33. al-Burūj (85) 21-22.

34. These terms are discussed in Ferdinand de Saussure, *Course in General Linguistics*, tr. Wade Baskin, New York: McGraw-Hill, 1965.

35. al-Tawba (9) 6.

36. al-Zukhruf (43) 3.

37. al-Baqara (2) 33.

38. al-Aʿrāf (7) 143.

39. al-Naḥl (16) 102.

40. al-Shuʿarāʾ (26) 193.

41. See Saḥīḥ al-Bukhārī (Kitāb al-waḥy), 2. See also Saḥīḥ Muslim (al-Faḍāʾil), 87; Sunan al-Tirmidhi (Manāqib), 7; Sunan al-Nasāʾi (Iftitāḥ), 27.

42. Abd al-Raḥman ibn Khaldūn, *The Muqaddimah: An Introduction to History*, tr. Franz Rosenthal, ed. N. J. Dawood, Princeton, NJ: Princeton University Press, 1987, pp. 338–9.

43. Vincent J. Cornell, *Realm of the Saint: Power and Authority in Moroccan Sufism*, Austin, TX, University of Texas Press, 1998, pp. 219–22.

44. Jean Cantein, *La Voie des lettres: Tradition cachée en Israel et en Islam*, Paris: Gallimard, 1981, pp. 35–6.

45. 'The Book of God's Word (the Bible) was a *speculum* [mirror] of the Book of his Work (nature)' – Jesse Gellrich, *The Idea of the Book in the Middle Ages*, Ithaca and London: Cornell University Press, 1985, p. 18.

46. Sir Thomas Browne, *Religio Medici*, Sect. 16 [1642], in M. R. Ridley, ed., *Sir Thomas Browne: Religio Medici and Other Writings*, London: Dent, 1965, p. 17.

47. The term 'visual language' was coined by the Anglican divine George Berkeley, who in 1733 wrote *The Theory of Vision, or Visual Language Shewing the Immediate Presence and Providence of a Deity Vindicated and Explained*, T. E. Jessop and A. A. Luce, (ed.), *The Works of George Berkeley*, London: Nelson, 1948–51, vol. 1, pp. 251ff.

48. Romans 1.19ff.

49. Cf. esp. Psalm 51.1-9.

50. In 603–15, Byzantine forces suffered a series of humiliating defeats, including the capture of Jerusalem in 614, at the hands of the armies of Shah Khusro II. Under the Emperor Heraclius, however, the 'Romans' from 622 staged a remarkable recovery, culminating in the recovery of Jerusalem in 630. This *sūra* is believed to have been revealed in 616.

51. Shiʾite theology teaches, in contrast, that the Qurʾān was created in time: cf. Moojan Momen, *An Introduction to Shiʾi Islam*, New Haven, CT: Yale University Press, 1985, p. 176.

52. David B. Burrell, CSC, 'Aquinas and Islamic and Jewish Thinkers', in Norman Kretzmann and Eleonore Stump, (ed.), *The Cambridge Companion to Aquinas*, Cambridge: Cambridge University Press, 1993, p. 61.

53. Muhammad al-Sakhāwī, *al-Maqāṣid al-Ḥasana*, Beirut, 1985, p. 642.

54. Harry Austryn Wolfson, *The Philosophy of the Kalam*, Cambridge, MA: Harvard University Press, 1976, p. 244.

55. Toshihiko Izutsu, *Ethico-Religious Concepts in the Qur'ān*, Montreal: McGill University Press, 1966, pp. 200–2.

56. Hasan Askari, *Alone to Alone: From Awareness to Vision*, Leeds: Seven Mirrors, 1991, p. 113.

57. Al-Qāḍī 'Iyāḍ al-Yaḥṣubī, ed. M. Amīn Qara 'Alī et al., *al-Shifā' bi-ta'rīf ḥuqūq al-Muṣṭafā*, Damascus: Dār al-Wafā', 1972, I, p. 207.

58. Sharaf al-Dīn al-Būsiri, *al-Kawākib al-Durriyya fī madḥ khayr al-bariyya*, Cairo: Dār Mansūr, 1334AH, p. 24.

59. For *al-Shāfī* as a name of the Prophet, see Annemarie Schimmel, *And Muhammad is His Messenger: The Veneration of the Prophet in Islamic Piety*, Chapel Hill: University of North Carolina Press, 1985, passim.

60. Alexandra Marks, *Christian Science Monitor*, November 25, 1997.

61. Shems Friedlander, *Rumi: the hidden treasure*, Louisville, KY: Fons Vitae, 2001, p. iv.

62. Annemarie Schimmel, *The Triumphal Sun: A Study of the Works of Jalaluddin Rumi*, Albany: State University of New York Press, 1993, p. 288.

63. A. Karabasoglu (ed.), *Çesitli ilahiler*, Istanbul: Seref Yayincilik, 1967, p. 202.

64. Muslim, Munafiqin, 40.

65. Jean-Marie Gaudeul and Robert Caspar, 'Textes de la tradition musulmane concernant le *taḥrīf* (falsification) des Écritures', *Islamochristiana* 6 (1980), pp. 61–104.

66. 'Imrān corresponds to the biblical Amram, Exodus 6.20.

67. For an account of the differing views of two influential commentators, cf. Sahiron Syamsuddin, '*Muḥkam* and *Mutashābih*: An Analytical Study of al-Ṭabarī's and al-Zamakhsharī's Interpretations of Q.3:7', in *Journal of Qur'ānic Studies*, I/1 (1999), pp. 63–79.

68. In Arabic, the concepts of 'without beginning' (*qadīm* or *azalī*) and 'without end' (*bāqī* or *abadī*) are clearly distinguished, while 'eternity' in Christian vocabulary has tended to embrace both.

69. Centring on the Arian controversy of the fourth century in Christianity, and the Mu'tazilite controversy of the ninth century in Islam. Both Arians and Mu'tazilites taught that the 'Word of God' was a created being, and both sought the aid of the state to uphold their views over against the orthodox insistence on the uncreatedness of the Word.

70. The term is used and explained by Harry Wolfson, *The Philosophy of the Kalam*, Cambridge, MA: Harvard University Press, 1976, p. 246.

71. Mahmoud Mustafa Ayoub, 'The Word of God in Islam', in Nomikos Michael Vaporis (ed.), *Orthodox Christians and Muslims*, Brookline, MA: Holy Cross Press, 1989, p. 73.

Chapter 3   Legacies of the past, challenges of the future

1. 'In appealing to Gen 15.6 in support of his contention that Abraham was not justified on the ground of works and has no right to glory before God, Paul was deliberately appealing to a verse of Scripture which his fellow Jews generally assumed to be clear support for the diametrically opposite view' – C. E. B. Cranfield, *A Critical and Exegetical Commentary on the Epistle to the Romans*, Edinburgh, T. & T. Clark, 1975, Vol. I, p. 229.

2. For an incisive survey of the problems of this vocabulary from a Jewish perspective, see Alon Goshen-Gottstein, 'Abraham and "Abrahamic Religions" in Contemporary Interreligious Discourse: Reflections of an Implicated Jewish Bystander', *Studies in Interreligious Dialogue*, 12/2 (2002), pp. 165–83.

3. For example, within the classical Lutheran tradition.

4. al-Nisā' (4) 34.

5. Cf. Muḥammad 'Abduh and Muḥammad Rashīd Riḍā, Tafsīr al-Qur'ān al-ḥakīm (Cairo, 1907-34) – cited in Hemut Gätje, *The Qur'ān and its Exegesis*, Oxford: Oneworld, 1996, pp. 248ff.

6. Abdullahi an-Na'im, *Toward an Islamic Reformation: Civil Liberties, Human Rights and International Law*, Syracuse, NY: Syracuse University Press, 1990.

7. Phyllis Trible, *God and the Rhetoric of Sexuality*, Philadelphia: Fortress Press, 1978; repr. 1985, p. xv. [Page references are to reprint edition.]

8. Zablon Ntahmburi and Douglas Waruta, for example, have used the terms 'hermeneutics' and 'interpretation' both interchangeably as well as distinct from one another. See their 'Biblical Hermeneutics in African Instituted Churches', in Hannah W. Kinoti and John M. Waliggo (eds), *The Bible in African Christianity: Essays in Biblical Theology*, Nairobi: Acton Publishers, 1997, p. 40ff.

9. K. Grobel, 'Interpretation', *Interpreter's Dictionary of the Bible* Vol. 2 (E–J), Nashville, TN: Abingdon, 1962, pp. 718–21.

10. Grobel, 'Interpretation'.

11. Johannes Philip Gabler, in an academic address which he delivered in 1787, argued that biblical theology needed to be emancipated from dogmatic theology since the two theologies had different tasks. Whereas the task of the dogmatic theology was normative, that of biblical theology was descriptive. Gabler was successful in convincing the academia of his day of the validity of his argument, and thus became the emancipator of biblical theology. For an English translation of the relevant portion of the text of Gabler's address see Ben C. Ollenburger, Elmer A. Martens and Gerhard F. Hasel, *The Flowering of Old Testament Theology*, Winona Lake, Indiana: Eisenbrauns, 1992, pp. 492–502.

12. Itumeleng J. Mosala, *Biblical Hermeneutics and Black Theology in South Africa*, Grand Rapids, MI: William B. Eerdmans Publishing Company, 1989. Another African scholar, Laurenti Magesa, has put forward his defence of a socio-centric biblical hermeneutics against what he calls a 'privatized' hermeneutics. See his 'From Privatised to Popular Biblical Hermeneutics in Africa', in Kinoti and Waliggo, *The Bible in African Christianity*, pp. 25–39.

13. E. A. Obeng, for example, argues for the usefulness of biblical criticism (historical-critical method) for the study of the Bible in the African context. See his 'The Use of Biblical Critical Methods in Rooting the Scriptures in Africa', in Kinoti and Waliggo, *The Bible in African Christianity*, pp. 8–24. For a Western defence of historical-critical method and critique of liberative hermeneutic, see T. E. Van Spanje, 'Contextualisation: Hermeneutical Remarks', *Bulletin of the John Rylands University Library of Manchester*, vol. 80, no. 1 (Spring 1998), pp. 197–217.

14. Isabel Apawo Phiri, *Women, Presbyterianism and Patriarchy: Religious Experience of Chewa Women in Central Malawi*, Blantyre: CLAIM, 1997; Mercy Amba Oduyoye, *Daughters Of Anowa: African and Patriarchy*, Maryknoll, NY: Orbis, 1995; Musimbi Kanyoro and Nyambura Njoroge, *Groaning in Faith: African Women in the Household of God*, Nairobi: Acton Publishers, 1996.

15. Mercy Amba Oduyoye, 'Introduction to the Proceedings', in *Transforming Power: Women in the Household of God: Proceedings of the Pan-African Conference of the Circle of Concerned African Women Theologians*, M. A. Oduyoye, ed., Accra-North, Ghana: Sam-Woode Ltd., 1997, pp. 4–6.

16. Phyllis Trible, 'Feminist Hermeneutics and Biblical Studies', in Ann Loades, *Feminist Theology: A Reader*, London: SPCK, 1990, p. 23.

17. Elizabeth Schüssler Fiorenza, *Bread Not Stone: The Challenge of Feminist Biblical Interpretation*, Boston: Beacon Press, 1984, p. xiii.

18. Phyllis Trible, *Texts of Terror: Literary-Feminist Readings of the Biblical Narratives*, New York: Fortress Press, 1984.

19. Fiorenza, *Bread Not Stones*, p. xvii.

20. Teresa Okure, 'Feminist Interpretations in Africa', in E. S. Fiorenza (ed.) *Searching the Scriptures* Vol. 1, London: SCM Press, 1993, p. 77.

21. Mercy Amba Oduyoye, *Hearing and Knowing: Theological Reflections on the Christianity in Africa*, Maryknoll: Orbis, 1986, p. 147.

22. Musimbi Kanyoro, 'Bible studies at the convocation', in Mercy Amba Oduyoye and Musimbi Kanyoro (eds), *Talitha Qumi: Proceedings of the Convocation of African Women Theologians, 1989*, Ibadan: Daystar, 1990, pp. 52–3.

23. Teresa Okure, 'Women in the Bible,' in *With Passion and Compassion: Third World Women: Doing Theology*, Virginia Fabella and Mercy Amba Oduyoye (eds), Maryknoll, NY: Orbis, 1988, p. 56.

24. Teresa Okure, 'The significance today of Jesus' Commission to Mary Magdalene', *International Review of Mission*, 81/322 (1992), pp. 177–88.

25. Musa Dube, *Other Ways of Reading: African Women Reading the Bible*, Geneva: WCC, 2001.

26. Musa Dube, *Post-colonial Feminist Interpretation of the Bible*, St Louis, MI: Chalice Press, 2000.

27. Musa Dube, 'Fifty years of Bleeding: A Storytelling Feminist Reading of Mark 5:24–43', *Ecumenical Review* (1998).

28. Musimbi Kanyoro, 'Engendered Cultural Hermeneutics as Key to the Liberation of Women in Africa', in *Ministerial Formation*, WCC Education Ecumenical Formation 86 (July 1999), pp. 52–3.

29. Musimbi Kanyoro, 'Feminist Theology and African Culture', in *Violence Against Women*, Grace Wamue and Mary Getui (eds), Nairobi: Acton Publishers, 1996, p. 5.

30. Musimbi Kanyoro 'Cultural Hermeneutics: An African Contribution', in Ofelia Ortega (ed.), *Women's Visions: Theological Reflection, Celebration, Action*, Geneva: WCC Publications, 1995, pp. 18–28; 'Engendered Cultural Hermeneutics as a Key to the Liberation of Women in Africa', in *Ministerial Formation*, 86 (July 1999), pp. 51–5.

31. Wamue and Getui (eds), *Violence Against Women*, pp. 13–20.

32. *Violence Against Women*, pp. 27–39.

33. *Violence Against Women*, pp. 40–8.

34. Mary Getui, 'The Grandmother in the African Traditional Household', in *Transforming Power*, Mercy Amba Oduyoye (ed.), Accra: Sam Woode, 1997, pp. 96–101.

35. Douglas Waruta and Hannah Kinoti, *Pastoral Care in African Christianity*, Nairobi: Acton Publishers, 1994.

36. Elizabeth Amoah (ed.), *Where God Reigns: Reflections on Women in God's World*, Accra: Sam-Woode, 1997, pp. 3–9.

37. Oduyoye and Musimbi (eds), *The Will to Arise: Women, Tradition, and the Church in Africa*, Maryknoll, NY: Orbis, 1992.

38. According to tradition, this verse was delivered in response to the question asked by one of the Prophet's wives: 'Why are men mentioned in the Qur'ān and we are not?' – al-Ṭabarī, quoted in Fatima Mernissi, *Women and Islam: An Historical and Theological Enquiry*, Oxford: Blackwell, 1991, p. 118.

39. Proverbs 2.16-19; 5.2-14; 7.6-27; 9.13-18.

40. This sentence is quoted on several conservative Christian websites, including 'Sovereign Grace Ministries', 'Grace Tabernacle', and 'Grace to You', attributed to the Nonconformist commentator Matthew Henry (1662–1714). I have been unable to track the original reference.

41. Galatians 3.28.

42. The 'secular' tone of Proverbs is shown by the fact that the book does not in fact speak about cultic participation by either men or women. The traditional position of orthodox Judaism is that women, because of the duties of child-rearing and home-making laid on them, are exempted from those commandments (such as congregational prayer) which need to be fulfilled at a specific time. See, for example, Jeffrey Cohen, *Horizons of Jewish Prayer*, London: United Synagogue, 1986, p. 156. It has been argued that the notorious morning prayer 'Blessed are you, Lord our God, King of the Universe, who has not made me a woman' could be seen as an expression of this dispensation, which might be seen as a kind of freedom.

Chapter 4   Scripture and the Other

1. Exodus 19.5.
2. Isaiah 45.1.
3. Exodus 20.10; 23.12.
4. Deuteronomy 27.19.

5. Deuteronomy 24.19.
6. Deuteronomy 16.11; 10.18.
7. Exodus 22.21.
8. Exodus 23.9.
9. Jeremiah 14.8.
10. Mathew 12.39ff.
11. Luke 11.29ff.
12. 1 Peter 2.9-10.
13. Luke 6.27.
14. Luke 14.15ff.
15. Luke 6.37.
16. Luke 9.49-50.
17. Matthew 15.24.
18. Notably, Proverbs 8, Ecclesiasticus 24, Wisdom 7.
19. Ecclesiasticus 1.1-10, 14-20.
20. Wisdom 7.22ff.
21. Hebrews 1.3.
22. John 14.6.
23. John 1.1ff.
24. al-'Alaq (96) 1-5.
25. M. Asad, *The Message of the Qur'ān*, Gibraltar: Dar Al-Andalus, 1984, pp. 963ff.
26. al-Baqara (2) 1-4.
27. al-Nisā' (4) 171.
28. al-Mā'ida (5) 65.
29. al-Mā'ida (5) 68.
30. Āl 'Imrān (3) 59-61.
31. Martin Lings, *Muhammad: His Life Based on the Earliest Sources*, Vermont: Inner Traditions International, 1983, p. 324ff.
32. Matthew 12.38ff., Luke 11.29ff. The Matthean reference expands Jonah's significance to be also (through his three-day sojourn in the belly of the fish) a sign of the resurrection.
33. Cf. Jane McAuliffe, *Quranic Christians: An Analysis of Classical and Modern Exegesis* Cambridge: Cambridge University Press, 1991.
34. Akbar reigned from 1542 to 1605. His religious project seems in part to have been inspired by a mystical experience in 1575, but it also served to magnify his own cultus and that of the imperial dynasty.
35. On the concept of different religious ends, see S. Mark Heim, *The Depth of the Riches: A Trinitarian Theology of Religious Ends*, Grand Rapids, MI: Eerdmans, 2001.
36. The conclusion offered by al-Ghazālī (1058–1111) in *Fayṣal al-tafriqa bayn al-Islām wa'l-zandaqa*, cited by Tim Winter, 'The Last Trump Card: Islam and the Supersession of Other Faiths', *Studies in Interreligious Dialogue*, 9/2 (1999), pp. 133–55.

37. For a Christian reflection on this theme of the curtailment of prophetic responsibility, see Kenneth Cragg, 'Magnificat – Allāhu akbar', pp. 21ff., in Michael Ipgrave, ed., *The Road Ahead: A Christian–Muslim Dialogue*, London: Church House Publishing, 2002.

38. Mohammad Hashim Kamali, *Principles of Islamic Jurisprudence*, Cambridge: Islamic Texts Society, 1991, pp. 149–68.

39. This threefold classification dates back to Alan Race, *Christians and Religious Pluralism*, London: SCM Press, 1983; 2nd edn, 1994.

40. Perhaps most trenchantly, Gavin D'Costa, *The Meeting of Religions and the Trinity*, Maryknoll, NY: Orbis, 2000.

41. An interesting reflection on the history of the modern use of the term, and its limitations, can be found in Nicholas Lash, *The Beginning and the End of 'Religion'*, Cambridge: Cambridge University Press, 1996.

42. *Shorter Oxford English Dictionary*, 'tolerance'.